EDUCATION AND HUMAN RELATIONS

The Library of Congress has catalogued this publication as follows:

Library of Congress Cataloging in Publication Data

Montagu, Ashley, 1905–
    Education and human relations.

    Reprint of the ed. published by Grove Press, New York.
    1. Education--Philosophy.   2. Interpersonal
relations.   I. Title.
[LB885.M6 1973]   370.19'3   72-11333
ISBN 0-8371-6659-4

Education
and
Human
Relations

by ASHLEY MONTAGU

GREENWOOD PRESS, PUBLISHERS
WESTPORT, CONNECTICUT

Acknowledgments

The journals and books in which most of the articles included in this volume were originally published are given below. To the publishers and editors of these journals and books I owe thanks for permission to reprint.

Democracy, Education, and Race. *School and Society,* vol. 59, 1944, pp. 227–229.

The Improvement of Human Relations Through Education. *School and Society,* vol. 65, 1947, pp. 465–469.

New Frontiers in Education. *School and Society,* vol. 74, 1951, pp. 309–311.

Teaching, Living, and Loving. *Why Teach?* D. Louise Sharp, ed., Henry Holt & Co., New York, 1957, pp. 161–162.

Art, Curriculum, and Culture. *Progressive Education,* vol. 31, 1954, pp. 181–185.

Our Changing Conception of Human Nature. *Impact* (Unesco), vol. 3, 1952, pp. 219–232.

Freedom of Inquiry and the Shared Experience. *Educational Freedom in an Age of Anxiety,* Gordon Hullfish, ed., Harper and Brothers, New York, 1953, pp. 70–81.

Time-Binding and the Concept of Culture. *Scientific Monthly,* vol. 77, 1953, pp. 148–155.

Man—And Human Nature. *American Journal of Psychiatry,* vol. 112, 1955, pp. 401–410.

Anthropology and World History. Twentieth Yearbook of the National Council for the Social Studies, vol. 20, 1949, pp. 217–227.

Reprinted by Greenwood Press,
a division of Williamhouse-Regency Inc.

First Greenwood Reprinting 1973
Second Greenwood Reprinting 1975

Library of Congress Catalog Card Number 72-11333

ISBN 0-8371-6659-4

Printed in the United States of America

Dedicated to the Memory of

MARIE I. RASEY

Great Teacher and Friend

Contents

Contents

Preface

The theme that runs through this little book is that education must consist in the training in the theory and art of human relations, and that all else in which human beings may be educated must be secondary to this primary purpose. In order to understand the meaning of human relations, it is necessary to have some grasp of the facts of human nature; unless we know what man is born *as,* it is not likely that we shall understand what he is born *for.* For that reason, many of the essays included in this volume are devoted to the discussion of the nature of human nature.

With one exception, the chapters of this book were originally published as separate articles, on different occasions and at different times, but in each one I have been anxious to present a particular viewpoint. That viewpoint is the same throughout the book; hence, as might be expected, there is a certain amount of repetition of ideas and of factual citation. It would have been a simple task to eliminate the repetition, but I have desisted from such editing for several reasons. In the first place, I like the repetition because it serves to emphasize the points I desire to make. In the second place, I believe it will be helpful to the reader to have these points repeated again and again; and in the third place, I have been anxious to retain the original integrity of the separate pieces, for purposes of reference, exactly as they appeared in the journals and books in which they were published. Except for bringing up to date the references and making some indicated stylistic improvements, the text has been left exactly as it was written.

The interest which some of these pieces created when they were originally published emboldens me to hope, now that they are together in book form, that they will find a wider and sympathetic audience.

ASHLEY MONTAGU

Princeton, New Jersey
June, 1957

1. Democracy, Education, and Race

The teachers of the young are at once the most important and the most privileged of all those agencies which enter into the functioning of society. Theirs is the most fundamental of all creative social functions; for what can exceed in social importance the task of molding the mind and helping to form the character of the growing member of society? The adult is, to a very large extent, what his teachers have made him, and in this very real sense, the true, unacknowledged legislators of any land are its teachers. There are many among us who owe whatever humanity they may have arrived at, and whatever claim they may have to the ability of using their minds critically, to the influence of a few childhood teachers; and I am afraid that there are those among us, too, who have suffered more pain and misery under the inflexible minds of too many unsympathetic teachers than they would perhaps care to recall. But it is as necessary to recall such unfortunate experiences as it is to recollect those happier ones which have meant so much to us, for there can hardly be a more immediate method by which to prove to ourselves the superlative value and importance of the sympathetic teacher.

In our democracy the purposes and methods of education have perhaps received more critically intelligent and experimental consideration than has been the case in any other country in the world, and as one important consequence of this it is now coming to be generally recognized that the educative process consists of much more than merely drawing out what is within each individual and filling him up with a lot of heterogeneous information. Reading, writing, and arithmetic are important—but not indispensable. A competence in such subjects by no means equips the individual to lead the life of an adequate human being or confers upon him the ability to be socially sympathetic to, and individually interested in, other human beings, of whatever country, caste, or color they may be. Indeed, a strong case might be made out for the claim that the three R's make it possible for an individual to be less of a human being with them than he would have been without them.

Indeed, what do the mass of people do with their ability to read and write and add up a column of figures? What, presumably, they have socially learned to do. They buy their morning newspapers as an addict buys his opium, there to read the day's calendar of murders, rapes, lynchings, fires, kidnapings, political chicanery, municipal holdups, and so on. Is it not a sufficient commentary upon the educational system of our schools when we reflect that tens of millions of individuals, of their own free will, every day purchase and read the kind of papers that they do? Who can observe mature individuals enchanted by the fantastic puerilities of the "funnies" without being convinced that somewhere something is somehow wrong? The ability of such individuals to write is used for all sorts of purposes, perhaps the strangest being to prove their literacy at a voting booth. While their ability to add up a column of figures they would seem to use chiefly for the purpose of scoring up the number of runs or touchdowns made during the season by their particular heroes.

This is, of course, a very one-sided and somewhat exaggerated picture, but does it not touch off something of the essential truth? The truth that education is for us, as human beings, valueless unless it is informed by the principle of humanity? For what is the use of any education unless it renders the individual capable of thinking, feeling, and knowing that nothing which is human is alien to him? Can we ask for a more tragic exhibition of antihuman behavior than we are at present witnessing, when members of the same society turn against one another for no offense greater than the fortuitous association of an individual with a particular religion or a difference in skin color? Such behavior usually goes by the names of religious or race prejudice or religious or racial intolerance. We have already seen, and some of us have experienced, the extremes to which such prejudices may be made to go in Europe. Can such things happen here? Certainly—but it must be our task, as teachers of human beings, to see that they do not. As teachers we can do a great deal toward making humanity safe for the world. Perhaps we cannot do everything, but we can do the most essential part of the spadework.

Right here and now we can introduce into our schools the long overdue teaching of the facts concerning race. These are simple and clear enough, and there is nothing in the least recondite or mysterious about them. It is through the lower- and upper-grade schools that the most significant work can be done in clarifying the minds of individuals concerning the facts of race, and in educating them in the proper attitudes of mind toward that subject. Let us teach geography, but instead of presenting facts of geography in the customary manner, let us humanize its teaching and furnish its field with the living peoples who inhabit this earth. Let us teach our pupils and students what we know concerning the peoples of the earth, and make clear their respective value for one another and their potentialities for civilization as a whole. Relations between other human beings and ourselves form the most important of all the experiences and situations of our lives. Would it not be incredible, did we not know it for a fact, that in our society human beings are permitted to enter into such relations without being equipped with the most elementary understanding of the nature of such relations? Certainly little or no attempt is made to supply them with the facts relating to race as made available by science; but we do, on the other hand, supply them with the kind of information which provides fertile ground for the development of race prejudices.[1] Here then, is a most important

[1] See E. V. Baker, *The Historical Outlook*, February, 1933.

field in which a great and valuable pioneer work demands to be done.[2]

But let no one be deceived into believing that, by teaching the simple facts of race, the problems of race will thus be automatically solved. Tolerance of other human groups, like all tolerance, is a matter of simple human decency; and decency is an attitude of mind which is, for the most part, culturally produced. Whether races or ethnic groups are biologically equal or not is an utterly irrelevant consideration where tolerance as an attitude of mind is concerned. Where differences exist between peoples it is surely obvious that tolerance ought to increase in proportion to the magnitude of the differences which are believed to exist between ourselves and others. The truly humane mind not only insists upon the right of everyone to be different, but rejoices in most of those differences and is not indifferent to those which it may dislike. Difference and variety in human beings is the salt of life and the basis of collective achievement. Until this is realized and such an attitude of mind becomes part of the heritage of every individual, no amount of instruction in the biological facts concerning "race" will ever succeed in eliminating race prejudices. Race prejudice can ultimately be regarded as merely the effect of a poorly or incompletely developed personality. If race prejudice is ever to be eliminated from our society, then, society must assume the task of educating the indivi-

[2] For a tentative program, most interestingly set out, see *The Teaching Biologist*, vol. 9, 1939, pp. 17–47; also M. F. Ashley Montagu, *Man's Most Dangerous Myth: The Fallacy of Race,* Harper, New York, 1952.

dual, not so much in the facts about "race" as in the processes which lead to the development of a completely integrated human being. The solution here, as in so much else, lies in education. Education for humanity first and above all else, and in the facts afterwards. For what is the use of facts unless they are humanely understood and intelligently used?

Here lies the great opportunity for those unacknowledged legislators of the world, the teachers of our young.

2. The Improvement of Human Relations Through Education

In our schools we teach the three R's; the fourth R, relations, human relations, it has been said, we do not teach. I think this is no more true than to say that what is wrong with most Americans today is that they have no values. Unfortunately, the trouble with most Americans is not that they have no values, but that they have too many values of the wrong kind. Similarly, it is not true to say that we fail to teach human relations in our schools. We do teach such relations not only in a negative way, but we teach them in an unmistakably positive way. And it is, on the whole, a way which is of the most unfortunate kind.

In our schools organized instruction in human relations, when it is not left to the coach on the football or baseball team, is generally more honored in the breach than in the observance. But unorganized instruction in human relations occurs in all schools. From the principal to the janitor, children learn how to behave in relation to others. Not so much from what they say, as from what they do.

Example is stronger than precept, and imitation is the most immediate form of learning. Words have no meaning other than the action they produce. And in our schools words are activated by what the teachers believe. From every standpoint, then, it is important that teachers, the unacknowledged legislators of the world, shall believe in the right things. For unless they do so, their words and conduct, no matter how noble the sentiments they are supposed to express, will be recognized for the counterfeit coin that they are. There are today thousands of teachers in our schools who are teaching race prejudice to their pupils. They do this not by means of prepared courses in the subject, but by their attitudes on any matter in which human relations arise, by a look, an expression, an inflection of the voice, or the weighting of a word. Though they have never been formulated in so many words, the views of such teachers on the subject of race and race relations are clearly understood by, and exert a considerable influence upon, their pupils. Such teachers do not belong in a school. The principal function of the teacher is, or should be, to help prepare the child for living a humane and co-operative life, not to infect his mind with the antihuman virus of racism.

No one should ever be permitted to become a teacher of the young unless by temperament, attitudes, and training he is fitted to do so. The teacher is the most important of all the public servants of the community; for what service can be more important to the community than the molding of the mind and conditioning of the social behavior of the future citizen? The anything but princely stipends with which he is rewarded for his services suggests that our society does not recognize the true value or function of the teacher.

The school, in America, is a place of instruction. It is not really a place of education in the proper sense of that word. In conformity with the requirements of a burgeoning industrial civilization, techniques and technology are at a premium. What can be used to succeed in such a society becomes that which is most emphasized during the learning period; the rest is sheer luxury, "frills," "school-larnin'," "academic stuff," or simply "points." From such a standpoint it is but natural that Americans should come to believe that the function of the school is essentially to teach the three R's in terms of the crude needs of an industrial civilization.

Clearly, values here are sadly mixed. They are the values of the world's largest industrial civilization. The value "success" in such a civilization is measured in terms of dollars. A man's worth in such a civilization is not his quality but his quantity, quantity of dollars, possessions.

Validation of success in terms of externals has become the mark of our civilization. In such a value system, human relations take on the ethical values of the salesman. To succeed you must know how to win friends and influence people, you must be "a good mixer," you must have lots of "contacts," and you must be able to "sell" people. The idols of the market place reign supreme. Competition is the most powerful law of the land. The competitive personality governed by the ideals of an industrial society must always be out in front. He must be better than others, for to be so yields the greatest returns. In the world of a person so conditioned it is taken for granted that some persons are inferior to others in their capacity to achieve. To most such persons the notion that there are whole groups of mankind which are unimprovably inferior is not only acceptable but indispensably necessary, for it constitutes at once a proof of the validity of the system and an incentive to go ahead and reap its benefits. It is a fully fledged belief in the doctrine of the survival of the fittest. The fit are those who are going to succeed or who have already succeeded, while the unfit are those who are not going to succeed, and it is, of course, most convenient and useful to know beforehand who is, and what groups of men are *not,* going to succeed.

It will readily be seen that the doctrine of racism is admirably adapted to the practices of imperialism and to the requirements of a ruggedly individualistic competitive society, "a graduated democracy," as one sociologist cynically put it. Not that such doctrines are indispensable correlates of such political and social practices; they do, however, provide the most convenient rationalizations for such practices, and, even if they are known to be untrue, they are nevertheless well found.

The very large amount of mental disorder, nervous tension, conflict, fear, anxiety, frustration, and insecurity which occurs in American society is largely due to the invariable failure of the false values by which men seek to live. The fact is that men cannot live in competition with one another without breaking down under the strain, however often they may attempt to relieve themselves of their frustrations and anxieties by attacking their scapegoats.

Man is born for co-operation, not for competition or conflict. This is a basic discovery of modern science. It confirms a discovery made some two thousand years ago by one Jesus of Nazareth. In a word: it is the principle of love which embraces within it all mankind. It is the principle of humanity, of one world, one brotherhood of peoples.

The measure of a person's humanity is the extent and intensity of his love for mankind. That measure is not the extent or intensity of his knowledge of the three R's. We all know to what a pass our knowledge of the three R's has brought us in a value system in which technology is esteemed far above humanity. We have been brought to, and we stand now upon, the very brink of destruction. If mankind is to be saved, it can be done only by replacing the values of industrial technology with those of humanity, of co-operation, of love. It is only when humanity is in control, that technology in the service of humanity will occupy its proper place in the scheme of things. A most important and immediate task is to make the people understand this. It is the duty of everyone capable of doing so to undertake this task. There must be a complete revaluation and reorientation of our values.

The school, beyond all else, must be considered as a place of education in the art and science of being a human being, the practice of human relations. Let us recall here the words of Franklin Delano Roosevelt from the 1945 Jefferson Day Speech which, so tragically, he did not live to deliver:

. . . the mere conquest of our enemies is not enough.

We must go on to do all in our power to conquer the doubts and the fears, the ignorance and the greed which made this horror possible.

Today, we are faced with the pre-eminent fact that *if civilization is to survive, we must cultivate the science of human relationships*—the ability of all peoples, of all kinds, to live together and work together in the same world at peace.

Without neglecting the important influence which the home constitutes, I believe that the science of human relationships is best taught and learned in the schools. We must shift the emphasis from the three R's to the fourth R, human relations, and place it first, foremost, and always in that order of importance, as the principal reason for the existence of the school. It must be clearly understood, once and for all time, that human relations are the most important of all relations. Upon this understanding must be based all our educational policies. We must train for humanity, and training in reading, writing, and arithmetic must be given in a manner calculated to serve the ends of that humanity. For all the knowledge in the world is worse than useless if it is not humanely understood and humanely used. An intelligence that is not humane is the most dangerous thing in the world.

Our schools must become institutions for the teaching of the most capitally important of all accomplishments, the theory and practice of human relations. Teachers must, therefore, be specially qualified to teach human relations. The importance of their function must be recognized and suitably rewarded by a society anxious to encourage the entry of the best kind of people into the professional privilege of preparing human beings for the art of living. There can be no more important task than this. It is a task which demands qualities of the teacher of the highest order. He must be temperamentally fitted for his profession, and he should himself be an exemplar of the art of living and the practice of human relations. Children would learn more from such teachers than from all the factually informed instructors in the world.

Are these specifications visionary? I think not. Certainly they will not be achieved if we think so. I believe not only that they can be achieved, but that it is our moral duty to see that they are brought into existence. Palliative, piecemeal approaches are not enough. If we are to cure the disease we must attack its causes. The white man is sick, abominably sick. His sickness is such that it is easily made to express itself in race prejudice. And yet the white man is no more the cause of race prejudice than is the colored man. It is the condition of the society into which he is born that determines whether he shall be racially prejudiced or not. It is these conditions which must be changed. We now know the causes of the sickness. Let us, then, apply the remedy.

Prominent among these causes are the substitution of economics for humanity, the substitution of society for community, the substitution of competition for co-operation, the frustration of our children for the disciplined permissiveness which should be their right, of the piling up of unexpended aggressiveness within them, and the production of conflicts and insecurities incident to the structure of a competitive society, a society which, on the one hand, preaches brotherly love and, on the other, practices self-love and the denial of brotherhood.

Most human beings know that humanity, love, is the basic principle by which to live, yet in their everyday lives they, for the most part, practice the doctrine of self-love and are hostile toward all those whom they conceive to stand in the way of their successful attainment. The reason for this tragic disparity between what they know to be right and what they do is simply that the structure of this society is such that the life of the person becomes reduced to a competitive struggle for existence. Under such conditions men everywhere become nasty, brutish, and cruel. They become atomistic, selfish, individualistic. Under such a system they cannot do otherwise, for the first law of life is and has always been self-preservation, and if the individual will not do everything in his power to gain security for himself, who will? Well might he echo that Talmudic voice which said: "If I am not for myself, who will be for me? If I am for myself only, what am I? If not now—when?"

In such a society man lives for himself alone; he is forced to. The right of other persons to existence is acknowledged insofar as it contributes to his security. Those persons or groups who, for any reason whatsoever, may be conceived as constituting an obstacle to that achievement therefore evoke hostile and aggressive responses. Yet these same persons know from such religious training as they may have had that such conduct is wrong and evil.

Were the conditions provided for such persons to lead the good life in harmony with all men, can there be the least doubt that they would take full advantage of those conditions?

In order to live the good life it is first necessary to live. If the structure of society is such that it makes of life a struggle for bare physical existence, in which the person is left to sink or swim entirely by himself, there is little time and no incentive to lead the good life. In an industrial civilization, with its emphasis on success in terms of material values, success is generally achieved in material terms at the expense of truly human values.

In American society, in short, we do not encourage the development of goodness, because goodness is not what we are interested in. Goodness belongs to a frame of reference other than that in which we make our living. It belongs to the covert rather than to the overt part of our culture. What we must do is to enthrone goodness, human relations, in the place at present occupied by economics. The idols of the market place must yield to those of humanity. A society such as ours, in which human relations are submerged in the economic system, can rescue itself only by submerging its economy in the matrix of human relations.

And this is the task that the schools must undertake, no less than the rescue of man from his debasing enslavement to the principles and practices of an acquisitive society.

Those who would have us believe that almost everything in the world is determined by economics are wrong. Certainly if you build a society on economic foundations and you make the whole super-structure dependent upon those foundations, economic determinism will undoubtedly be a most influentially operative principle. But only in a society which is so structured. If you identify human nature with economics, with production, you make of man a commodity, and you create a system of material values which readily lends itself to exploitation. When you build your society upon the foundation of human relations, as so many nonliterate societies have done, the processes of getting a living are cooperative. No one does anything for gain, the profit motive is nonexistent, and the individual feels secure in that he knows that as long as there is anything to eat every member in the group will eat. The menace of insecurity is collectively eliminated, and individual destitution is unknown. The determinants of conduct in such a society stem from social organization and religion, from the human relations of the group, as do the determinants of economic behavior.

The motives of human beings everywhere are human, *not* economic. They are made to become economic only in societies in which "moneytheism" is the prevailing religion. If, then, we would establish a world of humanity, we must educate human motivations in terms of humanity and not of economics. We must remove economics as the dominant motive from human relations, and make human relations the dominant motive in economics.

Let no one be deceived. Unless Western man is able to release himself from the degrading tyranny of his enslavement to the religion of economics, he is as certainly doomed to self-destruction as all the portents indicate that he is. Man cannot live by bread alone. Physiologically, biologically, psychologically, and socially, he can retain his health and flourish only in love of and co-operation with his fellow man.

A profit-motive, economic-struggle-for-existence society is a predatory society, a class-and-caste society, a divisive society, in which each person is isolated, preying upon and preyed upon by others.[1] Economic security, power, and prestige are the objectives which determine the motivations of men in such a society. Under such conditions men attempt to limit the opportunities for successful achievement to themselves. Few succeed and most men are caused to fail. This is the chief result, as well as the cause, of class and caste distinctions. The frustration and aggressiveness so produced is enormous. Professor Robert K. Merton has brilliantly described the frustrative mechanism in our society:

It is only when a system of cultural values extols, virtually above all else, certain common symbols of success *for the population at large,* while its social structure rigorously restricts or completely eliminates access to approved modes of acquiring these symbols *for a considerable part of the same population,* that antisocial behavior ensues on a considerable scale. In other words, our egalitarian ideology denies by implication the existence of noncompeting groups and individuals in the pursuit of pecuniary success. The same body of success symbols is held to be desirable for all. These goals are held to *transcend class lines,* not to be bound by them,

[1] Since this passage has been cited as evidence of my "socialistic or communist" tendencies, I should, perhaps, make it clear that I am not a socialist, that I abhor communism, and that politically I am a Jeffersonian democrat.

yet the actual social organization is such that there exist
class differentials in the accessibility of these *common*
success symbols. Frustration and thwarted aspiration
lead to the search for avenues of escape from a culturally induced intolerable situation; or unrelieved am-
bition may eventuate in illicit attempts to acquire the
dominant values. The American stress on pecuniary
success and ambitiousness for all thus invites exaggerated anxieties, hostilities, neuroses, and antisocial behavior.[2]

Race prejudice and discrimination are among the
consequences of such anarchic conditions, and these
racial hostilities will not be removed until these conditions are removed. Hence, let it be clearly understood that teaching of the facts of race in the schools
and elsewhere, intercultural programs, Springfield
Plans, and the like, while they may help as palli-
atives, will not substantially solve the problem,
though they may contribute toward its solution. The
problem we have to solve is first and foremost the
problem of how we can rebuild our society in terms
of human values in which human relations are given
a chance to function as they should. No matter what
we teach in the schools concerning the equality of
man, unless those teachings are provided with a social
milieu in which they can be practiced, they will wilt
and die in the breasts of those who are forced to
adapt themselves to the world as they find it.

How, then, is this problem to be solved?

The answer is: Through social engineering. Who
are to be the engineers? The answer to that is: The
children who are to be the adult members of the

[2] *American Sociological Review*, vol. 3, 1938, p. 680.

next generations. How are they to be prepared for their task? By being taught as clearly and as soundly as possible what the nature of our society is, why it must be modified, and how it can be changed, and this must constitute part and parcel of their training in human relations. Thus, at once will they be equipped with the reason and the means of bringing about the new dispensation of man.

This must be our program, courageously and un-equivocally expressed, for our cause is in the interest of every human being, of all mankind. There can be no nobler cause. It is up to the educators of America not only to be its standard bearers but with the co-operation of the enlightened part of our citizenry to undertake its realization.

There will be opposition and there will be diffi-culties, but opposition and difficulties exist in order to be overcome. Nothing was ever achieved without trying. And each of us who is in a position to can begin by trying to introduce these ideas in our com-munities. Tact, discretion, conviction, and, above all, courage will be required. On our side we start with some handicaps, the greatest of these being inertia and the fear of failure. But we must remember that we have the greatest of all advantages on our side: First, that our cause is sound, and, in addition, the consciousness of modern man that all is not well either with himself or with the world, and his desire for a better life.

Our task is to convince those who need to be con-vinced of the soundness of our cause and the benefits which will accrue to all men from its adoption. In-telligently planned and properly presented, I have

little doubt that it will earn the support of a sufficient number of persons to enable it to get away to a
good start.

The problem of race relations is simply one aspect
of the whole problem of human relations. If we
would have happy race relations, we must have happy
human relations, and if we would have happy human
relations, we must have a society based on human
relations. This, therefore, is what we must work to
achieve. All else must be considered as subordinate
and ancillary to this main task.

We know the problem; we know the solution. Let
us then ask ourselves the question: Are we part of
the problem or are we part of the solution?

3. New Frontiers in Education

I believe that one of the most important developments in our time for the educator is the discovery of culture. I mean the culture that is the domain of the anthropologist—not the "culture" that so many people talk about and so few seem to possess. I believe that that kind of culture, that private civilization of the person which we sometimes call his personality, will be assisted to become a reality when educators have fully grasped the significance of the anthropological conception of culture. What, then, is the anthropological conception of culture?[1]

To begin with a brief definition, the shortest and the best I know: Culture is the way of life of a people. It is a people's ideas, sentiments, religious and secular beliefs, its language, tools, pots and pans, its institutions. It is largely what makes a human being out of the organism perhaps too prematurely defined as *Homo sapiens*. Culture achieves this extraordinary

[1] It is ably discussed by L. A. White in his *The Science of Culture*, Farrar, Straus, New York, 1949. See also A. L. Kroeber and C. Kluckhohn, "Culture: A Critical Review of Concepts and Definitions," Papers of the Peabody Museum of Archaeology, Harvard University, vol. 47, 1952, pp. ix–223.

feat owing to the fact that this creature called *Homo sapiens* is equipped, not so much with a unique capacity, as with a capacity which is developed to a uniquely high degree, namely, the capacity to use symbols. This highly developed capacity or potentiality for symbol usage is one of the species characters of man, but it is not this symbol-using capacity which makes him the kind of human being he is capable of becoming. The other distinctively human trait is man's plasticity, his educability, the fact that he is born pretty much free of that instinctive equipment which in lower animals so largely predetermines their responses to their environment. Man has to learn his responses—if he does not he fails to develop any which are recognizably human. The fact is that you have to be taught to be human. The potentialities for being human may be there, but, if they are not humanly stimulated, conditioned, and organized, they do not develop a human form. The stimulator, the conditioner, and the organizer of human potentialities is culture.

This represents one of the most important discoveries made by man *for* man in the entire history of man. Consider what it means. It means that men can make of man anything that, within the limits of what is human, they desire. It means that human beings are *not* predestined by their so-called biological heredity to be what they become, but that they largely become what their social heredity conditions them to become, socializes or culturizes them to become. It means that human nature is not what is biologically given, but it means rather the organization by a cultural process of what is biologically given to function in a particular series of social ways at an increasingly higher level of integration. Or put in plain English, human nature has to be acquired. Purely genetic potentialities will not of themselves produce human nature. This does not mean that the human organism is a *tabula rasa* in Locke's or any other sense, but it does mean that human nature is something that we, as human beings, can, at least, have the major part in making.

This fundamental statement presents to educators the challenge of the most newly discovered frontier of knowledge. If man is so malleable, so plastic, so educable an organism, then the challenge and the choice are squarely before the educators of the world: To stop instructing and to begin discovering and thinking about the kind of human nature it is best for human beings to have. For it should be clear to everyone that it is critically important that, because man is so impressionably plastic a creature, because he is so precariously dependent for his development as a human being upon others, we be quite sure we know what kind of a human being we want him to become. That is one thing, but it is not enough. We must be quite sure that we fully understand the means of helping him to become so. Those of you who have read George Orwell's important and terrifying novel *1984* will have obtained a good idea of the kind of automata it is possible, under certain forms of socialization processes, to make of human beings. Orwell gives a perfectly sound description of the manner in which human beings could be turned into automata. Because man is so educable, so plastic a creature, he is constantly in danger of being harmed, of harming himself, and of harming others. It is therefore vital for us to discover whether there are any universally applicable laws in the organism potentially human which may help us to understand how it should be educated in order to function at its optimum as an harmonic human being.

And this is where the second great advance upon a new frontier has been made. This may be termed the discovery of the directiveness of human development. This discovery is the joint contribution of anthropologists, biologists, psychoanalysts, psychiatrists, and psychologists. It is so recent a discovery that I am not sure it is known to more than a small proportion of the members of the professions I have just named, and it is probably known to still fewer persons outside these professions. So perhaps we had better speak of this discovery as one in process of being made.

This discovery is that the organism potentially human requires to be socialized (that is to say, humanized, turned upon the lathe of human experience into a human being) in a very special way. What is that way? It is the way of love. The organism requires, demands, and must receive love. If it does not receive love it becomes disequilibrated and disharmonic. Its socialization, its educative process must be a loving one; otherwise it learns with great difficulty.[2]

What is love? And how has it come to be known that the organism potentially human must be loved if it is to develop harmoniously, creatively, and as itself a loving, co-operative human being? This

[2] Something of this seems to have been glimpsed in the psychologist-educator's law of reinforcement.

is like asking what electricity is, but there is no one who can really define it to the satisfaction of a physicist. We know how to make electricity, or at least to induce it, but it still defies definition. The best that a physicist can do is to define it in terms of the operations he uses to induce it operationally. And perhaps we can best answer the question, What is love? by stating: What the organism operationally demands in order to fulfill itself and develop as a harmonic human being.

The organism is born with certain basic needs which must be satisfied if it is to survive. These needs are: oxygen, food and liquids, bowel and bladder elimination, activity, rest, sleep, avoidance of pain and danger. It has been discovered that these basic needs must be satisfied in a dependency relationship such that the organism becomes increasingly aware of the fact that it is receiving its satisfactions whenever it requires them in a supportive manner; that it is being satisfied by persons who want to satisfy it, and who are—to put it in the best way I know—all for it; that it is being satisfied by persons on whom it can rely in the increasing awareness that its expected satisfactions will be met and not thwarted, that is to say, not frustrated. This is what every baby, every child, every adolescent, and every adult wants, and this is love. The synonyms are security, support, co-operation, the confidence that other human beings will support one actively and interestedly, the confidence that no one will ever willingly commit the supreme of all treasons against one, that is, to let one down when most needed.

We have learned, chiefly from the work of the

psychoanalysts, that it is the first six years that are critical here. The years during which the foundations of character and personality are being laid and solidified. This is the period during which the foundations are being laid for what may later develop as a harmonic personality or a neurotic. This is undoubtedly the most important period in the development of the human being as a person, the period during which he builds up his own ego, his own self, from the selves of others. As educators, therefore, this is the period to which, in the future, we must pay much more attention than we have in the past. And if we recognize the importance of this period for what it is, we shall see to it that the nursery school becomes part of the educational system of the land. It is during these first six years of life that the human being may be made or broken. We have learned this by following the socialization histories of many different persons and by correlating the details of their socialization with their traits of character and personality. Experimental studies, premeditated and unpremeditated, on lower animals and similar correlation studies on whole families, institution and noninstitution children, and on whole cultures have corroborated those findings.[3]

But the years of later childhood and adolescence have an importance of their own, for much of the good and much of the damage that may have been done during the preceding developmental periods may be undone in the succeeding periods. The growing organism, at all times, desires co-operation, and

[3] For the evidence, see M. F. Ashley Montagu, *The Direction of Human Development,* Harper, New York, 1955.

it needs this co-operation no less during one developmental period than another. The educator's task, then, should be clear: He must be a co-operator, a lover, an inspirer of confidence, and a drawer-out of the best that is within those whom he educates; and he must educate for co-operation, for community. For we know that persons who are not so educated are malfunctional, sick, inefficient, unhappy, anxious, and dangerous.

Biologists, social biologists, ecologists have shown us that contrary to the muscular Darwinian viewpoint, the drives to co-operation, to sociability, to community are present in all forms of life and are much stronger than what are generally considered to be competitive drives. The tough Darwinian viewpoint with its emphasis on competition is badly out of focus and is replete with misinterpretations of the evidence. The aggressive, hostile kind of competition which is associated with the Darwinian viewpoint, we now have good reason to believe, is produced only under certain conditions, conditions that may be resumed under the one rubric: *frustration*. Hostility, in fact, is love frustrated. Those who are not frustrated are not hostile. To be not frustrated one must have one's needs satisfied, one must be loved. Frustrating physical conditions can make one quite as hostile as those produced by persons. This is what the muscular Darwinians, and some of their modern successors, never realized, and so competition between animals, and by extrapolation from them to men, was set down as an innate drive. The evidence today strongly indicates that this is not true, and that it is almost certainly not true for man.

Children are not born selfish little egotists whose drives are mainly aggressive and competitive, "original sinners," evil, destructive creatures, brats who have to be "disciplined" into human beings by being sedulously and efficiently frustrated for the good of their actual or metaphoric souls. Aggressors are made not born.[4] On the other hand, the baby is born with drives which properly satisfied lead to co-operation. It is we, in our ignorance, who, failing to satisfy those needs, produce anxiety and hostility and then blame the child for being hostile! And so on at every stage of the process.

The biological drives toward co-operation, toward sociability, community, are part of the structure of protoplasm,[5] are demonstrably woven into the fabric of the organism. As educators it is this basic functional aspect of the organism that gives us the direction in which we must do everything we can to assist the development of the potentially human organism. The next great step which I foresee in the future of human education is the redefinition of its scope as the development of the organism potentially human in the science and art of being human, the remaking of our institutions of instruction in the three R's into institutes in human relations, in which the three R's are made part and parcel of the process of education in human relations, in humanity. For unless these "subjects" are humanized, of what further use can they be to mankind?

---

[4] See L. Bender's important study "Genesis of Hostility in Children," *American Journal of Psychiatry*, vol. 105, 1948, pp. 241–245.

[5] E. W. Sinnott, *Cell and Psyche*, University of North Carolina Press, Chapel Hill, 1950.

Man has lived long enough a victim of errors grown hoary with the ages, under the baleful influence of the false belief that man is naturally an egotistically competitive creature who must be disciplined and subdued. Man is born with potentialities for the development of the highest altruism, for altruism as a passion, for community, for ever-increasing creativeness, for unity—not for uniformity —for peace. As Martin Buber has said, genuine education of character is genuine education for community.[6]

[6] M. Buber, "The Education of Character," *The Mint*, Geoffrey Grigson, ed., Routledge and Sons, London, 1946, p. 14. For a further development of this viewpoint, see M. F. Ashley Montagu, *On Being Human*, Schuman, New York, 1950.

4. Teaching, Living, and Loving

Whenever I think, I shall remember who taught me how to think—so goes an old Spanish proverb, and so I think every day of my life. But I owe much more than the ability to think to my teachers; in large part I owe to them whatever capacity I have for living. My son is named after a beloved school-teacher of mine, and most of my books are dedicated to my teachers. The most important influence for good in my life have been my teachers, and any good that I may have done or may yet do in the world will be due largely, if not entirely, to the influence of my teachers.

In a world in which parents are often confused and bewildered, the education of children is often left to the teacher—and by education I mean not merely instruction in the three R's, but rather the drawing out of the potentialities of the child for being a human being competent in the art of human relations, in the ability to relate to other human beings. However deficient the educative processes may be in the home, a good teacher can often make all the difference. The compassionate teacher teaches the child the meaning of compassion, and the teacher who loves his or her children teaches them best. What, indeed, is the good teacher if not a well-informed, good lover?

My greatest teachers have been great lovers. The very interests I have in this world I can trace directly, in almost all cases, to the moments when my teachers with love and reverence spoke to us of some great figure or event. More than forty years after the event I recall, as if it were this morning, my teacher George Bidgood telling the story of the poet John Keats' life, and how I couldn't rest until I could get to the library (three miles away) and borrow the volume containing Keats' poems. The inspiration of that morning has been a continuous benison from that day to this. And so it has been with so many things.

No one better than I can know the truth that teachers are the most important and most valuable members of the community, for it is they who have the making of human beings in their hands in a manner somewhat distinct from the role which parents play in the lives of their children. Where parents are adequate, the teacher's task is so much easier. But parents are in many cases, alas, not going to be adequate, and this is where—within the warm orbit of his love—the teacher can make up for so much that the child would otherwise miss. To teach is to love. And in the final analysis, as Goethe said, we learn only from those whom we love. Hence, the primary qualification I would require of a teacher would be his ability to love—or failing that, his ability to learn how to love—the most important of all the qualities in the world. I must say that, as a teacher of almost a quarter of a century's standing myself, I have learned a great deal about the meaning of love from my students. I am indebted to them as my teachers as well as to those who were formally called my teachers. To lead and to cause to grow, to be led in turn and thus to grow oneself—what greater satisfaction can there be? Teachers are the unacknowledged legislators of the world; they are the instruments of purposes greater than themselves: the noble purposes with which they can inspire their pupils. What a challenge! What a privilege!

5. Art, Curriculum, and Culture

Art is one of the functions of human life, and it is of interest to note that there exists no record of a people, past or present, no matter how technologically primitive, that is without some form of art. Art as a necessity seems as vital to humanity as freedom itself. Art, indeed, is one of the great necessitators of freedom.

EXPRESSION IN THE GRAPHIC ARTS
CONCERNING BIOLOGICAL POTENTIALITIES FOR

In saying that art is one of the functions of human life, it is not being implied that art represents the realization of a biological drive or that there is such a thing as an art instinct. It *is* suggested that art constitutes the learned behavior of human beings by means of which, in a particular manner, they endeavor to embrace the world—to take what they can of it, and to give it what they are able of themselves.

To say that art does not represent the realization of a biological drive toward that activity is not the same thing as saying that art does not help one to realize one's biological drives. Indeed, the evidence is considerable that the practice of art and, to a lesser extent its appreciation, very significantly helps the person to a more efficient development of his biological drives or potentialities. If this is so, then the teaching of art becomes an indispensable part of the education of the human being.

It has been said that there is no drive or instinct-like tendency to art, but I am not so sure of that. Every infant I have ever studied exhibits clear evidences of an innate, unlearned capacity for harmony and rhythmic response to music. Furthermore, the same child will respond to different types of music in different, unlearned ways, resembling in an astonishing manner the adult dance forms which in each different culture are associated with the music of those cultures. It is no difficult thing to prove this fact for oneself experimentally. All that one needs is a number of records representing the dance music of different cultures, and a number of children in the vicinity of five years of age.

Quite evidently, human beings are born with potentialities for complex rhythmic responses to certain harmonic series of sounds. Conversely, rhythmic stimuli usually produce harmonic responses in the organism, a fact of which every mother who has rocked her baby to sleep has taken immemorial advantage. Lullabies do lull babies to sleep, and the fact that many adolescents are likely to pay more attention to what Billy Eckstine or some other redoubtable crooner has to say rather than to what their parents have to say suggests a possible whole new field of research here. Perhaps the things that cannot be said between parent and adolescent can be sung—sweetly and softly rather than in the fortissimo of feeling which usually prevails.

Of music it has been said that it utters those things which cannot be spoken. We have far from exploited for educational purposes the meaning of those words.

With respect to biological potentialities and the graphic arts, there is little or no evidence to go on. There is the case of Meng, the juvenile gorilla of the London Zoo, who used to trace with his forefinger the outline of his own shadow cast on the wall. (I have a picture of him doing this.) This may be put one step anterior to the child's account of what she did when she made a drawing. When asked what she did when she drew, this little girl replied: "First I think, and then I draw a line around my think." [1]

Those who are acquainted with the art work of children know how freshly vital and intuitive they can be. In a much more profound sense than poetry, drawing, in all its forms, constitutes one of the languages of the imagination; and perhaps we need claim no more for it than that, though art as a potentiality would seem to express itself more easily than does that most important of all potentialities, namely, speech.

Just as speech enlarges the functions of human life for growth, so does art. What are the functions of human life? This is a question we must clearly answer for ourselves if we are to understand the place of art in life, and so within the school, curriculum, and culture.

[1] Quoted by Roger Fry in his *Vision and Design,* Chatto and Windus, London, 1920, p. 96.

THE FUNCTIONS OF HUMAN LIFE AND EDUCATION

The function of human life is to live it in realization of and in harmony with the potentialities for being a good human being. And the only true education, in my opinion, consists in enabling each person to realize those potentialities to the fullest as the unique person that he is and as a member of an ever-extending fellowship of persons. This is a very different type of education from that which still prevailingly passes as such. It cannot be too often pointed out that what today, for the most part, passes as education is actually nothing of the sort. It is not a drawing out, but a pumping in; it is instruction in how not to realize one's potentialities, a tying up rather than an unloosening, a rigidifying rather than a development of greater freedom. We must not continue to mistake this kind of instruction for education.

If, then, it be conceded that the function of education is to assist the person to realize his potentialities for being a good human being, it is very necessary, at the outset, that we be clear about the nature of those potentialities and equally clear about the nature of goodness. It is my belief that unless we understand the nature of human nature we cannot genuinely understand the nature of what it means to be a good human being. Without that understanding we cannot, as educators, as efficiently fulfill our task as we can with the benefit of such understanding. Understanding human nature as it is, we are in a better position to assist its actualization in the selves we are called upon to educate, and what is equally important, we are in a better position to avoid committing those violences against the requirements of that human nature which are perpetuated in the name of education.

I have the privilege of being associated with a small but growing school, perhaps the most recent of all the schools, which can see no other way of interpreting the relevant evidence than that which leads to the conclusion that human beings are born good. Some literary and other critics have already referred to this school's interpretation of human nature as "the new Rousseauism," or "the new Kropotkinism," or as based on "a naive faith" in the goodness of human nature. I suppose one must expect this sort of thing, especially from those who, as Darwin once so charmingly put it, are in the utterly invulnerable position of not in the least understanding what they are talking about.

THE NATURE OF HUMAN NATURE

I have the greatest respect for Rousseau and Kropotkin, and I respect faith however naive, but my views are neither based on Rousseau, Kropotkin, nor have their origin in faith naive or otherwise. They are based on a scientific analysis of the facts relating to the nature of human nature as contemporary scientists have uncovered those facts. It is upon the basis of those facts and their interpretation that the scientific theory of human nature which has it that man is born good stands or falls. This theory is either true or false; whether it is the one or the other will not be established by calling it either kind or unkind names, but by dispassionate testing of its claims. In the presence of new ideas or startling opinions the truly scientific attitude is neither the will to believe nor the will to disbelieve, but the will to investigate.

This theory states that all human beings, with the few possible exceptions of those infants who as fetuses have had a bad time *in utero*,[2] are born without the innate aggressiveness which is customarily attributed to them, but with powerful drives which require satisfaction in terms of love. The evidence for the innate nonaggressiveness of human beings is based on the work of such students as Lauretta Bender[3] and Katherine Banham.[4] The evidence on the importance of love in the development of the person has recently been ably summarized in a World Health Organization publication by John Bowlby.[5]

From these and similar studies[6] it would seem that the most important of all the desires of a human being is the desire to be loved, and at the same time to love others. We have good evidence that aggressiveness comes into being only as a response to the

[2] M. F. Ashley Montagu, "Constitutional and Prenatal Factors in Infant and Child Health," *The Healthy Personality*, M. J. E. Senn, ed., Josiah Macy Jr. Foundation, New York, 1950, pp. 148–210.

[3] Lauretta Bender, "Genesis of Hostility in Children," *American Journal of Psychiatry*, vol. 105, 1948, pp. 241–245.

[4] Katherine M. Banham, "The Development of Affectionate Behavior in Infancy," *Journal of Genetic Psychology*, vol. 76, 1950, pp. 283–289.

[5] John Bowlby, *Maternal Care and Mental Health*, Columbia University Press, New York, 1951.

[6] M. F. Ashley Montagu, ed., *The Meaning of Love*, Julian Press, New York, 1953.

frustration of the expected satisfaction of love. As Ian Suttie was the first to point out in that fundamental and important work *The Origins of Love and Hate*,[7] aggressiveness is a mode of or technique for compelling the attention or love which has been withheld. Aggressiveness, therefore, is not something with which one is born, but rather something which is produced—produced by doing violence to the organism's needs and nature.

Upon this view, then, aggressiveness should not be regarded as a normal form of behavior confirming the doctrine of the original cussedness of human nature, but rather as evidence of frustration of some aspect of the need to be loved. If this theory is correct, then the best way of handling aggressive behavior is not in the time-honored manner with further aggression, but with what it calls for, namely, with understanding and love. Such studies as we have which bear on this subject tend to confirm the soundness of this theory.[8]

The General Implications of Human Goodness for Child Rearing, Art, and Education

I place great emphasis upon the findings that children are born without the kind of hostile aggressiveness which has so long been attributed to them, because once we drop the notion that children are

[7] Ian Suttie, *The Origins of Love and Hate*, Julian Press, New York, 1952.

[8] See F. Redl and D. Wineman, *Children Who Hate*, Free Press, Glencoe, Ill., 1951, and by the same authors, *Controls From Within*, Free Press, Glencoe, Ill., 1952.

born hostile little brats, we are likely to give a good deal more of the understanding love they need, and so much less of the "bringing up" that they don't need. Instead of exposing them to the regimen of systematic frustrations which we call "bringing them up," or "discipline," we will embrace them with the discipline of love, for which there can be no adequate substitute. The discipline of love has a firmness, a plasticity, and a warmth all its own.

Love is the biological birthright of every human being. It is not a chance development or an accident of being human, or something one prescribes, or something one deserves, or something one bargains for or purchases, or something one wins in a competition. Love is a need that every child which is born expects to have fulfilled, and it is a gift that can be given only when it is freely given. Human beings need to live by what is freely given them. Life itself is an unconditional gift, and so is love. And the love of lovers and the love of parents is the source of life. Loving personal relationships are the source of human life at conception; there is no substitute for such personal relationships at any other stage of life.

The way to produce warped, conflictful, warring human beings is to frustrate them as children. The way to produce warm, loving, peaceful human beings is by being warm, loving, and peaceful to them as children, to satisfy their need to grow in all these qualities as in others. To understand, and when one doesn't understand to go on loving—this is what is required. In our world of conflict in which human beings are bedeviled by neurotic feelings of guilt and responsibility, understanding and forgiveness implies a deep connection between human beings—a creative power to set one another free.

Free for what, it may be asked?

Free for the development of mental health, it may be answered, which has been defined as the ability to love and the ability to work.

And what part shall art play in the great liberation of man's potentialities to function in mental health? A great part, I should say, in helping the person not only toward self-expression, but what is perhaps more important, toward self-realization. Art is a technique for developing the self, of not merely growing but of increasing in complexity, and of learning critically to perceive and organize the world.

As a minimum, therefore, an education in the graphic and musical arts should form an indispensable part of the education of every human being—adapting, of course, such education to the aptitudes and abilities of each child. But this is a subject which I have very little competence to discuss beyond these generalities, and so I will turn to an aspect of art in relation to the curriculum, in which I feel somewhat more at home.

If we question ourselves concerning the purpose of the school curriculum, we may come up with several answers. My own answer would be that the purpose of all school curricula should be the education of good human beings, that this should be the primary purpose of all education, and that all else should be secondary to this. "Education," wrote Whitehead, "is the guidance of the individual towards a comprehension of the art of life. . . . Each individual embodies an adventure of existence. The art of life is the guidance of this adventure."[9] "Education is the guidance of the individual towards a comprehension of the art of life"—here we have explicitly set out in a single simple statement the functions of art, curriculum, and culture: guidance, comprehension, and the art of life.

And what is the art of life? Fundamentally, I believe it is the art of human relations. I am not suggesting that the art of life is exclusively the art of human relations, but that *fundamentally* it is. Humanity would suffer very great losses were its life restricted to human relations—but those losses are virtually as nothing compared to those which result from our lack of comprehension of the meaning of human relations. Furthermore, the evidence very strongly suggests that our appreciation of life suffers in direct proportion as our capacity for human relations has been arrested or disordered.[10] It is, of course, possible to develop high competencies and great creative genius in the appreciation and interpretation of various aspects of life even though one's capacities for human relations have been seriously disturbed, but it will generally be agreed that this is achieved at a tremendous cost to the individual and his colossal failure as a good human being. One thinks of such figures as Byron, Beethoven, Baudelaire, Gauguin, Rimbaud, Verlaine, Wagner, and in more recent times Scott Fitzgerald. The names that

[9] Alfred North Whitehead *The Aims of Education,* Mentor Books, New York, 1951, p. 46.
[10] Alfred Adler, *Social Interest: A Challenge to Mankind,* Putnam, New York, 1938.

could be added to these are many. Those I have referred to represent some of the people who came through with their creative abilities in spite of their disordered personal lives. How many human beings have there been who have not been able to break through the barrier of the disorder which has been created in them? Their number is legion.

Why should our conditioned capacity for human relations largely influence our capacity for experiencing life? Surely, it is because we mostly experience or perceive life according to the kingdom that has been created within us? [11] If this is so, then it should be clear that the most important thing in the world for human beings is to have a kingdom created within them which shall enable them optimally to comprehend the meaning of life and realize most beneficially the adventure of existence. It seems to me that the principal purpose of the school should be to help the child achieve these ends. These ends, in my view, can best be accomplished by completely revising our traditional conception of the school as the place of instruction in the three R's, and reconstituting it as a place of education—education in the genuine meaning of that word: helping the person to realize his potentialities for being a good human being. Not a place where twigs are bent or minds are molded, but where growing human beings are afforded the opportunities of their birthright: the supports, the stimulations, and encouragements for the optimum development of their potentialities for being good human beings. And this is where the

[11] M. F. Ashley Montagu, *On Being Human,* Schuman, New York, 1950.

opportunity should be afforded for education in the
most important of all the arts—the art of human
relations.

THE SPECIAL MEANING OF GOODNESS IN HUMAN BEINGS IN RELATION TO CULTURE, EDUCATION, AND ART

I have several times stated the function of education as being to help the person realize his potentialities for being a good human being, but I have
not yet defined what I mean by "goodness." As an
anthropologist and social biologist, examining the
history of man and observing man in his interpersonal relations, I have arrived at a definition of
goodness which I have found extremely helpful. I
believe it is a sound definition. I may be wrong. If
I am, at least let me have the courage to be wrong.
I offer it to you for what it is worth. Goodness is
that behavior which confers survival benefits upon
one's fellow human beings, survival benefits conferred in such a way as to contribute to the creative
development of one's fellow's potentialities for being
human.

And what does it mean to be human? It means
or should mean: to be a lover of one's fellow human
beings. And what is love? Love is the deep involvement of the self in others, and the conveying of that
feeling of involvement to others. It is the feeling of
profound emotional interest in others, the conveying
of that feeling, the feeling you inspire in others that
they can depend upon you, that you will support

them in their needs, and that you will never let them down, but that you will give them all the encouragements and stimulations and supports that it is within your power to give.[12]

For purely expository purposes, goodness and love are defined separately, but, in fact, goodness is but an aspect of love as love is an aspect of goodness. That is good which contributes to human welfare, and the forms of behavior which most efficiently contribute to human welfare are those which are best described as loving.

When we say, then, that the purpose of education should be to help the person realize his potentialities for being a good human being, we mean for being a loving person.

From the purely biological point of view, love for the human species is a function of the highest survival value. Adaptively it is the most efficient of all human qualities, and there can be not the slightest doubt that, whatever may have been the case in the past, the most significant test of fitness for humanity for the present and for the future is the ability to love.

To be human means not only to be the most educable of all living creatures, but the most capable of love. To be human determines the necessity of love, and we are coming to understand that to function

[12] See M. F. Ashley Montagu, ed., *The Meaning of Love,* Julian Press, New York, 1953; Nelson N. Foote, "Love," *Psychiatry,* vol. 16, 1953, pp. 245–251; Daniel A. Prescott, "Role of Love in Human Development," *Journal of Home Economics,* vol. 44, 1952, pp. 173–176; M. F. Ashley Montagu, *The Direction of Human Development,* Harper, New York, 1955; Erich Fromm, *The Art of Loving,* Harper, New York, 1956.

as a healthy human being means to function as a loving person. In this sense it should be the primary purpose of the schools to produce healthy human beings, and the school curriculum should be designed largely toward that end. There have been few schools since the days of Heinrich Pestalozzi (1746–1827) which have at all closely approached such a design for humanity.

It was Pestalozzi who said, "Love is the sole and everlasting foundation on which our nature can be trained to humaneness," and, "Without love, neither the physical nor the intellectual powers of the child will develop naturally. That is only human."[13] More than 150 years after these words were written, they have been dramatically corroborated by science down to the last detail. With the support of science and experience the design of a school curriculum for the production of good human beings should be the next major step in education.

Education, of course, begins in the home, and all reasonably envisaged school curricula should be organized in relation to the child and the world in which he lives. Part of that world is constituted by his home, parents, and siblings. I would therefore urge making the nursery school a part of the public educational system of the land; this, in order to bring both the children and the home under the influence of the school as early as possible. In this way the school and the parents can begin to co-operate in a mutually helpful and complementary manner on the education of the child. I would even go further and

[13] Heinrich Pestalozzi, *The Education of Man*, Philosophical Library, New York, 1951.

suggest that the state should make it obligatory for all prospective parents to attend school for two or three hours a week where they could receive expert instruction in the art of being good parents, and I would maintain this instruction until the child goes to nursery school.

Parents like teachers should be engaged in creative relationships with their children. We should no more abandon children to inadequate parents than we should abandon them to inadequate teachers. The way to make adequate parents, as adequate teachers, is through education. I think I have already indicated what that education should be.

True culture, it seems to me, lies in the cultivation of the qualities of being human—of loving-kindness, of the curious and active mind, and of receptiveness to beauty; in the realization that happiness is necessarily reciprocal and is found only in being given, that holiness is where love dwells and the promise of good, and in the understanding, as Lord Acton put it, that "liberty is not the power of doing what we like, but the right of being able to do what we ought."

The belief in progress, it has been said, is the wine of the present poured as a libation to the future. Progress is the product of those who have the wisdom to see the signs along the untrodden paths and the courage to tread those paths. We, as educators, are fortunate in that we already have the first crude road-maps of the direction in which we should go: toward a greater reverence for life and the recovery of creative freedom. The necessary theoretical knowledge, the science in its broad outlines, is already available; the practice of that knowledge, that is, the art, the art of human relations, remains mostly yet to be taught.

The greatest and most rewarding of all the arts is the art of living the good life. Is this art a possibility for human beings? It is a possibility, and education will make it a reality.

6. Our Changing Conception of Human Nature

Theories on human nature have been as numerous as the proverbial leaves of Vallombrosa, but it was not until the beginning of the twentieth century that human nature became a subject of serious scientific study. This study has revealed a multiplicity of facts which neither the theologians nor the philosophers so much as surmised. The facts set out in this article, and their discussion, should serve as a challenge to social thinkers and the leaders of public opinion.

WHAT IS HUMAN NATURE?

The answer to this question is the purpose of this paper. Obviously "human nature" can mean several different but mutually reconcilable things at one and the same time, so that until we have explored these different meanings and reconciled them, it will not be possible to make a brief, valid, and readily understandable statement as to the nature of human nature. However, it is possible to say several significant things about it at once.

First, then, it should be said that no organism of the species so prematurely named *Homo sapiens* is born with human nature. What human beings are born with is merely a complex of potentialities. Being human is not a status *with* which but *to* which one is born. Being human must be learned. This is an important distinction, for the age-old belief in the innate nature of human nature has been responsible for much personal, social, and political misunderstanding, and for an untold amount of human suffering.

What are the specific qualities or characteristics, and what is the peculiar nature, of man that distinguish him from all other creatures? On the basis of his obvious physical characteristics man is described as a mammal of the order Primates, genus *Homo,* and species *sapiens.* But what of his psychological classification? While every creature that is classified physically as man is thereby called *Homo sapiens,* no such creature is really *human* until it exhibits the conduct characteristic of a human being. If it is true that one has to learn the kind of conduct that is uniquely human, then any organism which fails to learn that conduct cannot be human. In a sense this is a sound argument, and a closer examination of this argument will serve to throw much needed light upon the meaning of human nature.

The fact is that man is human by virtue of both his physical and his mental traits. In the course of his evolution the two appear to have gone hand in hand. One can no more deny the status of being human to a newborn baby because it cannot talk, than because it cannot walk erect. The wonderful thing about a baby is its promise, not its performance —a promise to perform under certain auspices. A juvenile ape can do a great deal more than can a juvenile human [1],[1] but the promise of the child far exceeds that of the brightest of apes.

Now, what is this promise? The answer is: A remarkable capacity for learning to use complex symbols and symbol relationships [2], a "symbol" being a meaning or value conferred by those who use it upon any thing. A "sign," on the other hand, belongs to the physical world; it is a physical thing which indicates some other thing or event. A symbol belongs to the human world of meaning. Now, it is generally agreed that newborn babies are incapable of symbol usage; it is an ability which they have to learn; if they are not taught it they do not learn it.

We can thus say that human nature means the uniquely human set of *potentialities* for being human with which the organism *Homo sapiens* is born. *Potentialities* must be underscored, for what is generally erroneously assumed is that human beings are born with certain definite traits and characteristics which only need time if they are to develop, whereas the researches of the last thirty years have increasingly shown that the traits and characteristics of the organism will to a very large extent be determined by the kind of cultural stimulation which those potentialities receive.

What most persons have taken to be human na-

[1] The figures in brackets refer to the bibliography on pp. 79–83.

ture, is actually the *acquired* behavior of the person; this may and usually does become a second nature, and this, too, could be called human nature, since it is a function of man's nature in interaction with his environment. But it must not be confused with man's *inborn* nature—and this is exactly where the confusion is usually made. No doubt, since one always learns in a particular human environment, one's potentialities will develop according to the pattern of conditions to which they are exposed. Hence, human nature may express itself, or rather be made to express itself, in many different forms. But the differences in these forms are not, according to modern evidence, determined by innate factors but by environmental ones.

Man is born not with the ability to speak any language, but with a capacity or potentiality for speech, and this potentiality will never develop in the absence of the proper stimuli. These stimuli will usually assume a form determined by a particular environment, so that what the organism learns to speak will be of purely social origin, just as the way in which he learns to eat will be socially determined. Languages, knives and forks, and fingers, are all instruments for manipulating one's environment, but whereas fingers are natural, languages and knives and forks are artificial. Obviously it is no part of the primary or innate nature of man to create artifacts. Science knows of no natural drive in man to make knives and forks or to speak Italian; Australian aborigines neither use knives or forks nor do they speak Italian, not because they couldn't do so, but because they happen to be born into a cultural environment from which such instruments are absent and where their own language alone is spoken.

In short, how a person will behave, what he will do, think, or say, what language he will say it in, and what artifacts he will prize will be determined not by his innate nature so much as by his acquired experience. And this gives us the answer we have been seeking: Human nature consists of the unique potentialities for complex symbol usage with which the organism is born, potentialities which undergo development within the matrix of a stimulating cultural environment, the emergent result being a human being, made to measure, and tailored to the prevailing cultural pattern in which he has been conditioned. The process of learning the traditional cultural patterns is called *socialization,* and is essentially cultural in character. We may, then, call the natural endowment of human potentialities *primary human nature,* and the socialized development of those potentialities *secondary human nature.* Human nature, therefore, consists of both primary and secondary elements, the innate *and* the acquired. Where most errors have been committed in the past has been in the identification of the latter with the former.

While the primary human nature of all men is fundamentally similar, the secondary human nature frequently differs owing to differences in the history of cultural experience [3]. In short, human nature assumes secondary forms according to the pattern of the socialization process in which it has undergone development, and this pattern is determined by the cultural history of the group [4].

HUMAN NATURE BEGINS TO BE INFLUENCED
AT FERTILIZATION

In the tradition of Western civilization it is the custom to reckon age as beginning from birth; other civilizations, notably the Chinese, reckon age as beginning from fertilization or conception. Accumulating recent researches indicate that the latter is scientifically a much sounder manner of reckoning age than our own. The tendency to think of the child being born as a sort of *tabula rasa*, without a previous history, and beginning life, as it were, for the first time at birth, is unsound. The teaching in our scientific institutions hitherto has been that the fetus *in utero* is so carefully protected, so thoroughly insulated from virtually all stimulations originating in the mother or the outside world, that it develops autochthonously according to its own inner resources and the nutriment which it receives through the placenta. It was and is still being widely taught that since there is no nervous connection between mother and fetus, the mother's nervous states could not possibly influence the development of the fetus in any way.

With such a viewpoint concerning maternal-fetal relations, it is not to be wondered at that the prenatal period was considered irrelevant for the study of human nature. And yet nearly a century and a half ago a poet and thinker, Samuel Taylor Coleridge (1772–1834), wrote: "Yes—the history of a man for the nine months preceding his birth would, probably, be far more interesting, and contain events of greater moment, than all the three-score and ten that follow it" [5]. It has taken science 150 years to come somewhere near to supporting Coleridge's guess.

It is now a demonstrable fact that there is a very intimate connection between the nervous system of both mother and fetus; this connection is established through what is increasingly coming to be known as the neurohumoral system. This system is composed of the interrelated nervous and endrocine systems acting through the fluid medium of the blood (and its oxygen and carbon-dioxide content) [6].

There is good evidence that an emotionally disturbed pregnant woman may communicate her emotional disturbance, at least in chemical form, to her fetus. The Fels Institute workers at Antioch College, Yellow Springs, Ohio, have found that emotional disturbances in the pregnant mother produce a marked increase in the activity of the fetus. They have also found that fatigue in the mother will produce hyperactivity in the fetus; and that under severe emotional stress, especially during the later months of pregnancy, such mothers generally have babies who become hyperactive, irritable, squirming, feeding problems. Such an infant, says Sontag, "is to all intents and purposes a neurotic infant when he is born—the result of an unsatisfactory fetal environment. In this instance he has not had to wait until childhood for a bad home situation or other cause to make him neurotic. It has been done for him before he has even seen the light of day" [7].

Not only this, there is evidence that the mother's emotional disturbances are reflected, through disturbances in nutrition, in the skeletal system of the fetus [8]. It is, of course, not being suggested that the

mother's emotional states as such are transmitted to
the fetus—this is almost certainly not the case. What
does apparently occur is that the mother's emotional
disturbance manifests itself in impulses which, pass-
ing from cortex to thalamus and hypothalamus, proceed along the infundibulum to the pituitary gland.
The latter then secretes various hormones directly
into the blood stream which activate the glands of
the rest of the body, and since most, if not all, of
these hormones are of small enough molecular size,
they will pass directly through the placenta into the
fetus, or through the membranes surrounding it, and
there act upon it.

It is now well established that the fetus is capable
of responding to tactile stimuli, to vibrations, differences in pitch and tone, and to sound, to taste, and
to various gases [9]. In other words, it is clear that
far from being thoroughly insulated from the outside
world, the fetal organism is a great deal more sensi-
tive to it than we ever suspected.

Even more important than these is Spelt's remarkable discovery that the human fetus *in utero,* during
the last two months of gestation, can be conditioned
to respond to a paired stimulation of a vibrotactile
conditioned stimulus and a loud noise as uncondi-
tioned stimulus [10]. This is the first successful experimental attempt to condition the human fetus *in
utero.* Evidently, the fetus at seven months' gestation
age already has a sufficiently highly developed nervous system to be able to perform the operations
necessary for learning.

Greenacre thinks that the evidence indicates the
possible existence of pre-anxiety reactions in fetal

life without, necessarily, any psychic content [11]. She suggests that traumatic stimuli such as sudden sounds, vibrations, umbilical cord entanglements, and the like, including the "trip through the birth canal," may produce a predisposition to anxiety which, combined or not with constitutional traumatizing birth experiences, might be an important factor in the severity of any neurosis.

Without dwelling any further upon these facts, it should be reasonably clear that by the time a fetus is born it is highly probable that the genetic structure of its potentialities for being human has already been more or less greatly influenced by the environment in which it has undergone development, and that hence the primary human nature with which the organism *Homo sapiens* is born is not simply the genotypic potentialities as laid down at fertilization, but the more or less environmentally modified expression of those potentialities.

Such facts and their understanding, it will be readily granted, are of the first importance for the improvement of human welfare. The care of the child should, of course, begin with conception, and the best way of caring for the developing human being is by caring for the mother during and after her pregnancy.

HEREDITY AND ENVIRONMENT

Before proceeding further with the discussion, a few words must be said concerning the spurious dissociation between what is in fact only arbitrarily separable, namely, heredity and environment. Heredity is usually taken to mean the innate, i.e., the unadulterated biological inheritance of the organism as determined by the genes or hereditary particles in the chromosomes. This is usually referred to by geneticists as the *genotype;* the visible expression of the genotype is termed the *phenotype.* Now, the genotype always undergoes development within the complex medium of an environment, and the environment to a greater or lesser extent *always* influences the development of the phenotype. Hence, what the organism inherits is both the genotype and the environment which has formed it before birth. To disentangle what is due to genotype and what to environment, especially where behavioral traits are concerned, is a task beset with unsolved difficulties. What is, however, clear is that behavioral traits are due to a combination of genotypic and environmental factors with, by and large, environmental factors playing a dominant role. This by no means excludes genotypic factors, but it does suggest, other things being equal, that insofar as behavioral traits in man are concerned, man's social heredity plays a more considerable role than does his physical heredity.

Since, then, the heredity of a person consists of the interactive effects of the innate potentialities for development within the environment, it follows that where we control environment we to some extent control heredity. This is an extremely important conclusion, for it tells us that the most effective way for human beings, for some time to come, to influence the expression of the genotype is through the environment. Heredity in the genotypic sense may determine what we can do, but environment determines what we *do* do [12].

CONSTITUTION

In view of the recrudescence of a constitutional school of human nature, which attempts to link man's behavior to his physical traits [13], it is desirable here to say a few words concerning the conclusions reached by scientists with respect to the nature of constitution. Constitution may be defined as the sum total of the structural, functional, and psychological characters of the organism. It may be regarded as the integral of genetic potentialities influenced in varying degrees by internal and external environmental factors. Constitution is more properly regarded as a process than as an unchanging entity. It is not a biological entity, a structure predestined by its genotype to function in a predetermined manner. The manner in which all genotypes function is determined by the interaction of the genotype with its environment.

All the relevant researches indicate that every genotype is a unique physico-chemical system comprising particular kinds of potentialities having definite limits. These limits vary from individual to individual, so that were the genotype to be exposed to identical environmental conditions, its interactive expression would nevertheless continue to vary from individual to individual. In point of fact the environmental conditions are never the same for two individuals—a fact which renders it necessary for us to remember that heredity is not merely constituted by the genotype, but by the genotype as modified by the environment in which it has developed. The fact cannot be too often reiterated that what the organism inherits is a genotype *and* an environment, that heredity is the dynamic integral of both, the resultant of the dynamic interaction between the two.

Finally, it has become quite clear that genes, the hereditary particles carried in the chromosomes, do not determine either characters or traits; what they determine are the responses of the developing organism to the environment. The genes that the individual inherits are not, therefore, equivalent to predestination, but are amenable to the influences of the environment and hence, to some extent, to human control.

Where the constitutionalists go wrong is in their claim that "structure determines function." Function is, of course, an aspect of structure, but as any elementary student of physiology should know, *the functions of structures assume their particular character according to the environment in which they operate* [14]. The constitutionalists consistently fail to understand the importance of the environment, especially in human development, and this is the most fatal of all the criticisms of their work.

With What Kind of Behavioral Equipment Is Man Born?

It is generally agreed that man is born free of those biological predeterminants of behavior which

characterize other animals. Man is born without instincts [15], without those psychological dispositions
which cause other animals to respond in a particular
manner to a particular stimulus accompanied by a
particular emotion. The form of the animal's responses is predetermined; man has to learn the forms
which his responses assume. While other animals are
mostly creatures of instinct, man is the creature of
habit—the habit which he acquires from his culture.
But these habits are organized by his culture around
a number of urges, drives, or basic needs, as they
have been variously called. These terms are the mer-
est labels for physiological conditions, the exact nature of which is far from being known.

There is fairly general agreement as to the number
and definition of basic needs. A basic need may be
defined as a requirement of the organism which
must be fulfilled if the organism and the group are
to survive. The main basic needs are: oxygen, liquid,
food, activity, rest, sleep, bowel and bladder elimination, and avoidance of pain and danger. Malinowski
has defined the concept of basic needs as "the environmental and biological conditions which must
be fulfilled for the survival of the individual and the
group" [4]. It is important to note that this definition
includes the group as well as the individual, and this
inclusion constitutes one of the most significant de-
partures from, and improvements upon, the old concept of "instinct." It constitutes an explicit recognition of the fact that man, if not all other animals,
functions, if he functions at all, in relation to a
group; and that, so far as human beings are con-

cerned, functioning, that is behaving, apart from a group simply does not occur. When human beings behave socially it means that they have been socialized within a human group—if they have not been socialized within a human group, then they do not behave like human beings.[2] Indeed, the person becomes related to himself to the extent to which he becomes related to the group [16].

Malinowski, who was the first anthropologist to attempt a comprehensive theory of needs, set out the permanent vital sequences, as he called them, which are incorporated in all cultures, in a list from which we shall take only one impulse, as follows:

(a) *Impulse,*	(b) *Act,*	(c) *Satisfaction.*
Hunger,	Ingestion of food,	Satiation.

This kind of sequence is rather too elementary and, in fact, unsound, because Malinowski has failed to perceive that the act leading to satiation (here in the case of hunger) is an indissoluble part of the process of satisfaction, and because there is rather more involved in the actual sequences than Malinowski's order suggests. A list of basic vital sequences prepared by the present writer follows.

---

[2] There are no examples of completely isolated human children—in spite of many published accounts to the contrary—but there are several recorded cases of children who have been almost completely isolated from human contact for several years (these cases are discussed in M. F. Ashley Montagu's *The Direction of Human Development,* Harper, New York, 1955) ; such children fail almost completely to develop as human beings, and in many cases are even psychically blind and deaf, unable to walk or run, and unable to make more than the most elementary sounds.

Warning mechanism →	Physiological tension →	Urge or need →	Satisfaction	
			Which leads to →	Homeostasis
Accumulation of CO_2	Oxygen hunger	Intake air	Breathing	Oxygenation of tissues
Periodic gastric waves	Hunger	Ingest food	Ingesting food	Satiation
Dryness of mucous membranes	Thirst	Intake liquid	Intaking liquid	Quenching
Reduced organization	Fatigue	Rest	Resting	Restoration of muscular and nervous energy
Excess energy	Restlessness	Be active	Activity	Reduction of energy to equilibrium
Reduced energy	Somnolence	Sleep	Sleeping	Awaking with restored energy
Tonic disturbance	Bladder pressure	Micturate	Micturation	Tension removal
Peristalsis	Colon pressure	Defecate	Defecation	Tension removal
Autonomic activity	Fright	Escape	Escaping from danger	Relaxation
?	Pain	Avoid	Avoidance	Return to normal state
Cue	Internal excitation	Craving	Neuromuscular act	Equilibrium

The warning mechanism is a minimum physiological change which provides the organism with cues enabling it to anticipate the full effects of depletion or excess. Thus, we generally drink before we become conscious of intense thirst, and indulge in activity long before we feel any intense need for it, and we breathe long before we feel the phobic stir, which precedes each breath we take, so faintly that we do not normally notice it [17]. The warning mechanism or minimum physiological cue enables the organism to anticipate its needs before the latter become too disturbing. Forestalling behavior therefore becomes possible [18]. We are warned long before there is any tissue depletion or experience of excess. The intervals between the warning activity and biochemical depletion or excess vary, the margin of safety varying from a few seconds in respiration to hours in water balance. The greater the interval the longer are the psychological complications which can be developed. The extent to which psychological processes can influence the various warning mechanisms varies widely.

Since the warning mechanisms operate through a phobialike anxiety, failure to obtain the necessary satisfaction of the need which develops serves to increase anxiety; as Kubie remarks, every basic need functions between the pressure of "normal phobic and normal compulsive psychologic processes which are the Anlage of all pathologic distortions" [17].

Under certain conditions the warning mechanism and the basic need may become detached from one another; the warning mechanism in the form of a sense of dryness, for example, may continue to operate even though the tissues are thoroughly hydrated. Or vice versa, there may be a considerable degree of dehydration without any sense of dryness or thirst. Such dissociations are usually pathological. Anorexia or chronic lack of appetite is a well-known example.

One of the prevailing myths of our Western tradition is the belief that the baby is born inheriting something of the ancestry of its lowly forebears, with respect not only to its physical but also to its psychological traits. The alleged "aggressiveness" of animal nature, it has been held, is in part inherited by the young *Homo sapiens*. Freudian and Jungian psychology assumes the innate aggressiveness of man, and civilization is regarded by both as a more or less unsuccessful attempt to keep this innate aggressiveness within bounds [19].

Freud's postulation of a "death instinct" is now generally discredited, but his use of the synonymous term "the destructive instinct," still plays a considerable role in psychoanalytically influenced writings. This alleged "destructiveness" is identified with man's alleged inherited aggressiveness, and so one of the dominant views about human nature in our own day has become associated with the belief that man is inherently born aggressive.

For this viewpoint there is not a shred of supporting evidence. On the contrary, *all* the available evidence gathered by competent investigators indicates that man is born without any aggressiveness within him whatsoever. Professor Lauretta Bender, through whose hands have passed literally thousands of children, in her capacity as a child psychiatrist finds that, far from being inborn, hostility in the child "is a symptom complex resulting from deprivations which are caused by developmental discrepancies in the total personality structure, such that the constructive patterned drives for action in the child find inadequate means of satisfaction and result in amplification or disorganization of the drives into hostile or destructive aggression." "The child," she writes, "acts as though there were an inherent awareness of his needs and there is thus the expectation of having them met. A failure in this regard is a deprivation and leads to frustration and a reactive aggressive response."

Indeed, the development of the organism is toward maturation in terms of co-operation. Bender calls it "the inherent capacity or drive for normality." And she adds: "The emphasis on the inborn or instinctive features of hostility, aggression, death wishes, and the negative emotional experiences represents a one-sided approach which has led our students of child psychology astray" [20].

Professor Abraham Maslow makes much the same points in an important article. Maslow writes: "Those human impulses which have seemed throughout our history to be deepest, to be most instinctive and unchangeable, to be most widely spread throughout mankind, i.e., the impulses to hate, to be jealous, to be hostile, to be greedy, to be egotistic and selfish, are now being discovered more and more clearly to be acquired and *not* instinctive. They are almost certainly neurotic and sick reactions to bad situations, more specifically to frustrations of our truly basic and instinct-like needs and impulses" [21].

Professor Gardner Murphy writes: "As we watch behavior in early childhood, we no longer assume that each individual will inevitably push himself ahead and crave every toy or every attention he can get; instead, we begin to ask if there is something in our society that does not satisfy the child's needs and, therefore, makes it aggressive" [22].

The fact seems to be that aggressiveness usually

develops in the child as a result of frustration, that is to say, the blocking of expected satisfaction. The infant expects to have its needs satisfied; if those needs are not satisfied it feels frustrated, and normally reacts with aggressive behavior. It is now coming to be understood that aggression is, in effect, a technique or mode of compelling attention to, and satisfaction of, one's needs.[3] Such an interpretation of the meaning of aggressive behavior in children puts a very different complexion upon the manner of handling it than has been customary in the past. Aggressive behavior in all human beings most frequently represents a response to frustration [23]; a response to the frustration of expected satisfaction. In this connection the work summarized in Ashley Montagu's *The Direction of Human Development* [24], and more recently in the WHO report by John Bowlby on *Maternal Care and Mental Health* [25], should be consulted.

As a result of the work of a large number of investigators (whose research will be found described in the two last mentioned books) it is now indisputably clear that the satisfaction of the child's needs by the mother or some substitute for the mother is necessary for the healthy physical and mental development of the person. Physical satisfaction of the needs of the organism is not enough; what is necessary in addition is the warmth, the love of another

[3] I believe that the late Ian B. Suttie was the first to point this out in his important book *The Origins of Love and Hate,* Kegan Paul, London, 1935, Julian Press, New York, 1953. This book is, incidentally, perhaps the best and most original critique of Freudian psychoanalysis extant.

human being who is deeply interested in the welfare of the child.

It is becoming increasingly clear that the infant is born not only with the need to be loved, but also with a need to love; he is certainly not born with any need to be aggressive.

This view of human nature makes a very different picture from the traditional one, with its conception of man born with an aggressiveness which the process of socialization must suppress or eradicate. It is that view which rendered rationalizations about the "innate warlikeness" of man, and facile generalizations about man as a "brute," the stock in trade of every former authority on human nature. But modern research has shown that this view of human nature is erroneous. Man is not born evil or aggressive—he is rendered so. This being the case, it is incumbent upon us to realize that we can best change human nature for the better not by working on man's biological inheritance but by working on his social inheritance: by changing those conditions which produce disharmony in the person and corresponding disharmony in his society. As Profesor Warder C. Allee has said: "Despite many known appearances to the contrary, human altruistic drives are as firmly based on an animal ancestry as is man himself. Our tendencies toward goodness, such as they are, are as innate as our tendencies toward intelligence; we could do well with more of both" [26].

The school of evolutionary thought which preached the struggle for existence and the survival of the fittest gave a one-sided view of nature as a competitive "red in tooth and claw" process, and omitted almost entirely the factors of co-operation and mutual aid, which play so great a role in the ecology, the balance, of nature. The resulting view of nature was thus put badly out of focus, but upon it was erected a view of human nature which was as readily accepted as was the evolutionary theory of nature modeled on a *laissez-faire* industrial civilization.

Perhaps one of the most important of our conclusions is that never was there a stereotype more unsound than that enshrined in the view "You can't change human nature." On the contrary, we find that man is the most plastic, the most malleable, the most educable, of all living creatures; indeed, that educability is a species character of *Homo sapiens*. Man is the learning animal, and he is capable of learning and changing his views and his habits throughout his life.

Human nature, happily, is a great deal better in its promise than man has thus far realized in his performance.

BIBLIOGRAPHY

1. KELLOGG, W. N. and L. A., *The Ape and the Child,* Whittlesey House, New York, 1933; YERKES, R. M. and A. W., *The Great Apes,* Yale University Press, New Haven, 1934; BENCHLEY, B. J., *My Friends the Apes,* Faber and Faber, London, 1944; CATHY HAYES, *The Ape in Our House,* Harper, New York, 1951.
2. CASSIRER, E., *An Essay on Man,* Yale University Press, New Haven, 1944; WHITE, L. A., *The Science of Culture,* Farrar, Straus, New York, 1949, pp.

22–39; LA BARRE, W., *The Human Animal,* University of Chicago Press, Chicago, 1954.

3. BOAS, F., *The Mind of Primitive Man,* Macmillan, New York, 1938; MONTAGU, M. F. ASHLEY, *Man's Most Dangerous Myth: The Fallacy of Race,* 3rd ed., Harper, New York, 1952.

4. LINTON, R., *The Cultural Background of Personality,* Appleton-Century, New York, 1945; MALINOWSKI, B., *A Scientific Theory of Culture,* University of North Carolina Press, Chapel Hill, 1944; *Personal Character and Cultural Milieu,* D. G. Haring, ed., Syracuse University Press, Syracuse, 1957; SARGENT, S. S., *Culture and Personality,* Wenner-Gren Foundation, New York, 1949; KLUCKHOHN, C., and MURRAY, H. A., *Personality, in Nature, Society, and Culture,* Knopf, New York, 1953; COUTU, W., *Emergent Human Nature,* Knopf, New York, 1949; MONTAGU, M. F. ASHLEY, *On Being Human,* Schuman, New York, 1950.

5. COLERIDGE, S. T., *Miscellanies, Aesthetic and Literary.* Collected and arranged by T. Ashe, Bohn's Standard Library, London, 1885, p. 301.

6. MONTAGU, M. F. ASHLEY, "Constitutional and Prenatal Factors in Infant and Child Health," *The Healthy Personality,* M. J. E. Senn, ed., Josiah Macy Jr. Foundation, New York, 1950, pp. 148–210.

7. SONTAG, L. W., "Differences in Modifiability of Fetal Behavior and Physiology," *Psychosomatic Medicine,* vol. 6, 1944, pp. 151–154; SONTAG, L. W., and RICHARDS, T. W., "Studies in Fetal Behavior," *Monographs of the Society for Research in Child Development,* vol. 3, 1938, pp. x–72; SONTAG, L. W., "War and the Fetal Maternal Relationship," *Marriage and Family Living,* vol. 6, 1944, pp. 1–5.

8. SONTAG, L. W., and HARRIS, L. M., "Evidence of Disturbed Prenatal and Neonatal Growth in Bones of Infants Aged One Month," *American Journal of Diseases of Childhood,* vol. 56, 1938, pp. 1248–55.

9. MONTAGU, M. F. ASHLEY, "Constitutional and Prenatal Factors in Infant and Child Health," op. cit.;
CARMICHAEL, L., "The Onset and Early Development
of Behavior," *Manual of Child Psychology*, Wiley,
2nd ed., New York, 1954, pp. 60–185.

10. SPELT, D. K., "The Conditioning of the Human
Fetus *In Utero*," *Journal of Experimental Psychology*, vol. 38, 1948, pp. 338–346.

11. GREENACRE, P., *Trauma, Growth and Personality*,
Norton, New York, 1952.

12. DUNN, L. C., and DOBZHANSKY, TH., *Heredity, Race
and Society*, Mentor Books, New York, 1946; HAL-
DANE, J. B. S., *Heredity and Politics*, Norton, New
York, 1938; HOGBEN, L., *Genetic Principles in Medi-
cine and Social Science*, Knopf, New York, 1931;
JENNINGS, H. S., *The Biological Basis of Human
Nature*, Norton, New York, 1930; KALMUS, H., *Gene-
tics*, Pelican Books, London, 1948; MULLER, H. J.,
LITTLE, C. C., and SNYDER, L. H., *Genetics, Medicine,
and Man*, Cornell University Press, Ithaca, N. Y.,
1947; SCHEINFELD, A., *The New You and Heredity*,
Lippincott, Philadelphia, 1950.

13. HOOTON, E. A., *The Twilight of Man*, Putnam, New
York, 1939; *The American Criminal*, Harvard Uni-
versity Press, Cambridge, 1939; *Crime and the Man*,
Harvard University Press, Cambridge, 1939. See also
SHELDON, W. H., *The Varieties of Human Physique*,
Harper, New York, 1904; *The Varieties of Human
Temperament*, Harper, New York, 1942; *Varieties
of Delinquent Youth*, Harper, 1949. For a criticism
on the work of Hooton, see also MERTON, R. K., and
MONTAGU, M. F. ASHLEY, "Crime and the Anthro-
pologist," *American Anthropologist*, vol. 42, 1940,
pp. 384–408. For a criticism of Sheldon's work, see
SUTHERLAND, E. H., "Critique of Sheldon's *Varieties
of Delinquent Youth*," *American Journal of Sociology*, vol. 57, 1951, pp. 10–13; WASHBURN, S. L.,
"Physical Anthropology," *American Anthropologist*,

vol. 53, 1951, pp. 561–563; MONTAGU, M. F. ASHLEY, *The Biosocial Nature of Man*, Grove Press, New York, 1956.

14. NEEDHAM, J., *Biochemistry and Morphogenesis*, Cambridge University Press, New York, 1942; WADDINGTON, C. H., *Organizers and Genes*, Cambridge University Press, New York, 1940; BONNER, J. T., *Morphogenesis: An Essay on Development*, Princeton University Press, 1952; RUSSELL, E. S., *The Interpretation of Development and Heredity*, Clarendon Press, Oxford, 1930.

15. BERNARD, L. L., *Instinct, a Study in Social Psychology*, Holt, New York, 1924.

16. FROMM, E., *Escape From Freedom*, Rinehart, New York, 1941; *Man for Himself*, Rinehart, New York, 1947.

17. KUBIE, L. S., "Instincts and Homeostatis," *Psychosomatic Medicine*, vol. 10, 1948, pp. 15–30.

18. STAGNER, R., "Homeostasis as a Unifying Concept in Personality Theory," *Psychological Review*, vol. 58, 1951, pp. 5–17.

19. FREUD, *Beyond the Pleasure Principle*, Hogarth Press, London, 1922; *The Future of an Illusion*, Hogarth Press, London, 1928; *Civilization and Its Discontents*, Hogarth Press, London, 1929; *An Outline of Psychoanalysis*, Norton, New York, 1949. See almost any of Jung's works and those of his followers.

20. BENDER, L., "Genesis of Hostility in Children," *American Journal of Psychiatry*, vol. 105, 1948, pp. 241–245.

21. MASLOW, A. H., "Our Maligned Animal Nature," *Journal of Psychology*, vol. 28, 1949, pp. 273–278.

22. MURPHY, G., "Man and His Destiny," *The Nature of Man*, A. W. Loos and L. B. Chrow, eds., The Church Peace Union, New York, 1950, p. 62.

23. DOLLARD, J., et al., *Frustration and Aggression,* Yale University Press, New Haven, 1940.

24. MONTAGU, M. F. ASHLEY, *On Being Human,* Schuman, New York, 1950; *Darwin, Competition and Cooperation,* Schuman, New York, 1952; *The Direction of Human Development,* Harper, New York, 1955; GRAHAM, M., *Human Needs,* Cresset Press, London, 1951; ALLEE, W. C., *Cooperation among Animals,* Schuman, New York, 1951; HOLMES, S. J., *Life and Morals,* Macmillan, New York, 1948; *Explorations in Altruistic Love and Behavior,* P. A. Sorokin, ed., Beacon Press, Boston, 1950; SINNOTT, EDMUND W., *Matter, Mind and Man,* Harper, New York, 1957.

25. BOWLBY, J., *Maternal Care and Mental Health,* Columbia University Press, New York, 1951.

26. ALLEE, W. C., "Where Angels Fear to Tread: A Contribution from General Sociology to Ethics," *Science,* vol. 97, 1943, p. 351.

7. Freedom of Inquiry and the Shared Experience

It is often stated that America owes its greatness to the spirit of competition which characterizes its people. "Rugged American individualism," "the go-getter spirit," and other such phrases give implicit recognition to this idea. Commerce, it is said, through competition, is the lifeblood of a nation.

These ideas, I suggest, are erroneous, tragically erroneous. I suggest that such greatness as America has achieved it has achieved *not* through competition but in spite of competition, that the lifeblood of a nation is not competition, but social welfare through co-operation, that, indeed, commerce through competition can be the death of a nation, and that only through the dominance of the co-operative motive can any people or nation survive. Finally, I suggest that in a competitive society freedom of inquiry is not genuinely possible, that freedom of inquiry is proportional to the development of co-operation within any society, a society in which there is an absence of dictatorship of any sort, and the person is free to arrive at and express his own judgments without fear of punishment and in the expectation of the desire in his fellows to understand.

In view of the fact that there exists, at the present time, a widespread belief in a biological basis for competition, an idea that competition is a form of behavior with which every organism is born, it will be necessary to discuss such ideas in the light of the findings of scientific investigators during the recent period.

Just when the idea of the innate competitiveness of man came into being, it would be difficult to say. The idea is at least several thousand years old and was probably already bruited long before the Old Testament came to be written.[1] Possibly the idea of the innate competitiveness of man is as old as man himself. There are some existing nonliterate cultures, such as the Zuñi Indians of the Southwest, which abhor competition and in which the idea of innate competitiveness is nonexistent.[2] It is quite possible that many prehistoric peoples held similar views. But here we are largely in the field of conjecture. One thing, however, is certain: The scientific validation of the idea of the innate competitiveness of human nature was provided in the nineteenth century by Darwin and his supporters, particularly by Herbert Spencer and the school of Social Darwinists who followed his lead. Competition was the cornerstone of the whole edifice of the theory of evolution by means of natural selection. Darwin had himself

[1] See Kurt Singer, *The Idea of Conflict*, Cambridge University Press, New York, 1950.

[2] Ruth Benedict, *Patterns of Culture*, Houghton Mifflin, Boston, 1934, p. 127.

derived the concept of competition from the sociopolitical thinkers of the late eighteenth century, principally through the medium of Malthus' *An Essay
on the Principle of Population*.

The prevailing notion that Darwin influenced the
sociopolitical thinkers of the nineteenth century toward the development of Social Darwinism is only
partially true. In a very real sense the ideas which
were later termed "Social Darwinism" already enjoyed a certain currency even before the birth of
Darwin in 1809. The essential conception of natural
selection, the struggle for existence, that "strong and
constantly operating check," as Malthus put it, Darwin took, as he readily acknowledges in *Origin of
Species* (1859), from Malthus' *Essay* (1798). The
struggle for survival of a population increasing at a
geometric rate in a world in which the food supply,
according to Malthus, increased only at an arithmetic
rate, and in which war, pestilence, and famine are
the natural checks to human increase, renders competition inevitable and natural, even desirable, as
honest Malthus insisted. Hence, "commerce, through
competition, is the lifeblood of a nation." What
Darwin did was to take over lock, stock, and barrel
the ideas of Malthus—who applied them principally
to man—and apply them to the whole kingdom of
living things. Darwin simply translated the sociological language of his time into the language of
biology, so that "commerce, through competition, is
the lifeblood of a nation" became "evolution,
through competition in the struggle for existence,
is the lifeblood of the species."

What, in fact, Darwin and his supporters demonstrated to the satisfaction of most of their contemporaries was that competition is inherent in the nature of living things. At the height of the industrial revolution this was a demonstration which fitted the book of *laissez-faire* capitalism to perfection. It was accepted with enthusiasm. In the struggle for existence the fittest came out on top. Hence, the exploitation of labor was not only permissible but justifiable; "inferior and superannuated races" could be relieved of their lands and even exterminated; wars were justified in that they gave a biologically just decision, a natural arbitrament between peoples, and served as nature's pruning hook to keep her orchard healthy.[3] Theologians and educators were confirmed in their belief in the inherent naughtiness of man, and the notion that the brat has to have the inborn "evil" disciplined out of him and the "good" disciplined into him took on a deeper meaning than it had hitherto possessed. In the Freudian psychology—Freud was much influenced by Darwin —the inherent aggressiveness of man becomes a major instinct,[4] and for this reason Freud takes a rather gloomy view of man's future.[5]

[3] See George Nasmyth, *Social Progress and the Darwinian Theory,* Putnam, New York, 1916; Richard Hofstadter, *Social Darwinism in American Thought 1860–1915,* Beacon Books, Boston, 1955; M. F. Ashley Montagu, *Darwin, Competition and Cooperation,* New York, Schuman, 1952.

[4] Sigmund Freud, *Beyond the Pleasure Principle,* Hogarth Press, London, 1922; *An Outline of Psychoanalysis,* Norton, New York, 1949, pp. 21–23.

[5] Sigmund Freud, *Civilization and Its Discontents,* London, Hogarth Press, 1929.

This sentence had almost begun with the words "Contemporary scientific opinion is slowly veering away from such notions," but since this would not be a true description of what is happening, it should more accurately be said that some scientists, the very few, indeed, who have been considering the evidence as a whole, have come to the conclusion that competition and aggressiveness are not inherited forms of behavior but acquired ones, that Darwin, and especially his followers, by overemphasizing the importance of competition and neglecting the factor of co-operation in the evolutionary process, badly put the whole picture out of focus. And Freud followed him.

Competition and aggressiveness are, of course, observable facts of animal and human behavior, but in the sense in which these terms are generally understood and used—that is, competition as a contest, a striving against others to achieve goals, and aggressiveness as behavior calculated to inflict injury—neither competition nor aggressiveness are inborn patterns of behavior. Competition and aggressive behavior come into being only under certain conditions, and those conditions are largely, if not entirely, of a frustrative nature.[6] Frustration may be defined as the thwarting of an expected satisfaction. A certain amount of frustration is a necessary part of the development of every person. To learn to postpone immediate satisfactions for long-term ones requires

[6] See John Dollard, et. al., *Frustration and Aggression*, Yale University Press, New Haven, 1944; M. F. Ashley Montagu, *The Direction of Human Development*, New York, Harper, 1955.

the experience and handling of a certain amount of frustration, and this is both unavoidable and desirable if a healthy, mature personality is to be developed. But too much frustration is quite another thing. This is undesirable because it serves to cripple the development of a healthy personality, having the effect of producing either an excessively dependent, shy person or an overaggressive, highly competitive one.

Human cultures differ widely in the kind and amount of frustration to which children and adults are exposed. Significant differences in personality have been observed in correlation with differences in kind and amount of frustration to which children have been exposed in those cultures.[7] In general the rule is: The less frustration children have experienced, the better balanced and the less aggressive and competitive they are likely to be.[8]

So far as the nonhuman animal kingdom is concerned, the corrective to the Darwinian point of view has been given by Allee and his co-workers,[9] and by

[7] See Margaret Mead, ed., *Cooperation and Competition Among Primitive Peoples,* McGraw-Hill, New York, 1937; *From the South Seas,* Morrow, New York, 1939; Douglas G. Haring, ed., *Personal Character and Cultural Milieu,* University of Syracuse Press, Syracuse, 1957; John J. Honigmann, *Culture and Personality,* Harper, New York, 1954; R. R. Sears, et al., "Some Child-Rearing Antecedents of Aggression and Dependency in Young Children," *Genetic Psychology Monographs,* vol. 47, 1953, pp. 135–234.

[8] See C. Kluckhohn, H. Murray, and D. Schneider, *Personality,* Knopf, New York, 1954; Gardner Murphy, *Personality,* Harper, New York, 1947.

[9] See Warder C. Allee, *Cooperation Among Animals,* Schuman, New York, 1951; *Animal Aggregations,* University of Chicago, Chicago, 1931; W. C. Allee, et al., *The Principles of Animal Ecology,* Saunders, Philadelphia, 1949.

other biologists.[10] The work of these scientists confirms the conclusions put forward by Kropotkin in his famous book *Mutual Aid* (1902).[11] In the penultimate paragraph of their monumental work *The Principles of Animal Ecology*, Allee and his coworkers state this conclusion in the following words: "The probability of survival of individual living things, or of populations, increases with the degree with which they harmoniously adjust themselves to each other and their environment. This principle is basic to the concept of the balance of nature, orders the subject matter of ecology and evolution, underlies organismic and developmental biology, and is the foundation for all sociology."[12]

This is the principle of co-operation, and the evidence today indicates that it is the principle which is more dominant than that of competition in the evolution and survival of animal and human groups. While man is qualitatively different from nonhuman animals, the fact is that there is no validation to be found in the nonhuman animal kingdom for innate competitiveness and aggression. Even if this were not the case, man is unique and there is no necessity to demonstrate his noncompetitiveness on the basis of anything other than his own nature. Even if man were by nature competitive, which the evidence

[10] William Patten, *The Grand Strategy of Evolution*, Badger, Boston, 1920; S. J. Holmes, *Life and Morals*, Macmillan, New York, 1948; H. G. Andrewarth and L. C. Birch, *The Distribution and Abundance of Animals*, University of Chicago Press, Chicago, 1954; Th. Dobzhansky, *The Biological Basis of Freedom*, Columbia University Press, New York, 1956.

[11] Pëtr Kropotkin, *Mutual Aid: A Factor in Evolution*, Extending Horizons Books, Boston, 1955.

[12] Allee, et al., p. 729.

clearly indicates he is not, he is so plastic and malleable a creature[13] that he could as easily channel his competitiveness into co-operative and creative directions. But the fact is that man is born neither aggressive nor competitive. The best evidence we have on this matter comes from those who have actually studied the question at first hand. Thus, for example, Dr. Lauretta Bender, the child psychiatrist, from her experience with several thousand children writes that, far from being inborn, hostility or aggression in the child "is a symptom complex resulting from deprivations which are caused by developmental discrepancies in the total personality structure, such that the constructive patterned drives for action in the child find inadequate means of satisfaction and result in amplification or disorganization of the drives into hostile or destructive aggression." "The child," she writes, "acts as though there were an inherent awareness of his needs and there is thus the expectation of having them met. A failure in this regard is a deprivation and leads to frustration and a reactive aggressive response."

Indeed, the creativeness of the organism is directed toward maturation in terms of co-operation. Bender calls it "the inherent capacity or drive for normality." And she says, "The emphasis on the inborn or instinctive features of hostility, aggression, death wishes, and the negative emotional experiences rep-

[13] Th. Dobzhansky and M. F. Ashley Montagu, "Natural Selection and the Mental Capacities of Mankind," *Science,* vol. 105, 1947, pp. 587–590; Paul R. David and Laurence H. Snyder, "Genetic Variability and Human Behavior," *Social Psychology at the Crossroads,* John H. Rohrer and Muzafer Sherif, eds., Harper, New York, 1951, pp. 53–82.

resents a one-sided approach which has led our students of child psychology astray."[14] Charlotte Buhler,[15] Katherine Banham,[16] Abraham Maslow,[17] and others[18] have come to the same conclusion.

The essential condition of life is interdependency, and the organism called man is born in a state of dependency which requires interdependency if it is to survive. Babies expect to be co-operated with, and when they are so treated they co-operate. Witness the disappearance of the night-walking father attempting to calm the baby—babies no longer cry during the night because in recent years parents have learned a little how to co-operate with their babies during the day. If we can now teach parents how to co-operate with their children throughout their lives, we may yet succeed in producing well-balanced, co-operative human beings.

Educators may be expected to catch up with the biological and psychological evidence which will provide more than an illuminating insight into the natural bases for co-operative endeavor, but the time is short. There is an urgency about this learning of the essential facts which living in an atom-bomb

[14] Lauretta Bender, "Genesis of Hostility in Children," *American Journal of Psychiatry*, vol. 105, 1948, pp. 241–245; *Aggression, Hostility and Anxiety in Children*, Thomas, Springfield, Ill., 1953.

[15] Charlotte Buhler, "Spontaneous Reactions of Children in the First Two Years," Proceedings and Papers of the 9th International Congress of Psychology, 1929, pp. 99–100.

[16] Katherine Banham, "The Development of Affectionate Behavior in Infancy," *Journal of Genetic Psychology*, vol. 76, 1950, pp. 283–289.

[17] Abraham Maslow, "Our Maligned Animal Nature," *Journal of Psychology*, vol. 28, 1949, pp. 273–278.

[18] For a résumé of the evidence, see M. F. Ashley Montagu, *The Direction of Human Development*, Harper, New York, 1955.

world makes particularly pressing. Our splintered values have made the horrible, shattering reality of an atom-bomb world possible. If there are still men of good will alive—and I know that there are many—then it is up to them to acquaint themselves with the essential facts concerning human nature and to do something toward seeing that information realized toward the production of better human beings. Our present educational and social failure to recognize new bases of human relationships must change if we are to survive—it is nothing less than that.

Human beings who are torn and distracted by internal insecurities and anxieties, who are conditioned to compete on weekdays and to love their neighbors on Sundays, cannot long endure. A people made up of such persons must eventually founder on the rock of its own false values. External defenses can never make up for the lack of internal controls. What we need to do is to build internal controls in human beings so that they can withstand external pressures and maintain internal equilibrium. And this can never be done by doing violence to their nature. It can only be done by strengthening those basic needs with which all human beings are born—not by frustrating them. These basic needs are: oxygen, food, liquid, rest, sleep, activity, bowel and bladder elimination, escape from danger, avoidance of pain; together they add up, on the part of the organism, to the desire to be loved, the desire for co-operation. I have dealt with this subject at length in my book *The Direction of Human Development*,[19] from

[19] M. F. Ashley Montagu, *The Direction of Human Development*, Harper, New York, 1955.

which the reader may go on to verify the facts for himself.

The evidence seems to be clear that when the child's basic needs are adequately satisfied, when, in other words, the child is loved and a minimum of frustrations are produced in it, no matter in what culture or class that child grows up and develops it tends to be a well-equilibrated, nonaggressive, co-operative person.

We live by a pure flame within us; that flame is love. It is the source from which we draw and convey our warmth to others. It is the light which guides us in relation to our fellow men; it is the flame before which we warm the hands of life, and without which we remain cold all our lives. It is the light of the world. The light which it casts enables us clearly and unequivocally to see our relation to our fellow men. It is up to us to keep that flame burning, for if we fail to do that, there is a real danger that the light will go out of the world.

The critical social and educational problem of today is one of learning how shared relationships may be fostered and freedom of inquiry accelerated. It seems to me, first, that this must be done through the schools, and second, that there must be a complete change in the attitude toward education. In the United States at the present time we have little, if anything, resembling education. What we *do* have is instruction. What are we educating *for*? Obviously we are instructing our future citizens in what it takes to live in the world in which they find themselves. We are equipping them with the elementary skills, reading, writing, and arithmetic, which it takes to maintain that world. More by default than by design, we teach them a kind of cracker-barrel human relations; we teach them to become echoes, as it were, of other stereotyped lives already lived. That is to say, in the most important of all relations, human relations, as educators we fail most miserably. For what can be more important than human relations? What is all the instruction in the world worth if it is not accompanied and integrated by an understanding of man's responsibility to man? A scientific approach to education must begin with the basic assumption that values must in the long run be tested by their capacity to contribute to the happiness and creativeness of human beings living together. If we can find a scientific basis in *fact* for what *should be,* we should at least be willing to give it a try.

I suggest, then, that some of our schools be transformed into institutes or schools for the study of the science and art of human relations. I mean that children be taught the theory and practice of human relations from their earliest years, and for this purpose, among other things, I would make the nursery school part of the public educational system of the land. The three R's must be secondary to this primary matrix of human relations, for whatever is learned should be learned primarily with reference to its significance for human relations, and always with the emphasis on co-operation, on shared relationships. Children should be taught not how to become submissive echoes of their teachers and their traditions, but how to evaluate humanely and critically the world in which they are living. They should be taught not only the overt but also the covert values of their society, and they should be taught not only what is right with their society—that George Washington could not tell a lie—but also those things that are wrong with it, and that it is going to be their responsibility to put them right, and how they may be put right.

I am often asked how this undertaking can possibly be accomplished. Don't I realize the enormous social inertia or even active opposition with which one would have to contend if one attempted to develop such a program? What happened in Pasadena? Look at Bertrand Russell and City College. What about the Rugg textbooks? Yes, these are serious symptoms, but fortunately they are not exhibited throughout the United States. It would be wonderful if one could start with a community and work directly through the school system, and this should be our aim whenever and wherever possible, but failing that, a single teacher in a single classroom, multiplied over many schools, could do valuable work. This would not be enough if it stopped at a single classroom in a few schools, but the hope would be that, with constant awareness of the problem growing, the movement to teach human relations in the school would grow and spread.

As I have said, there is not too much time left. The tendency in the United States to equate economic liberty with democracy has helped to disguise the fact that many of our ideas and institutions are under constant threat from our very own selves, for persons who are in conflict with themselves, anxious and insecure, tend to be rigid in their ideas and in their behavior, as if to lean upon their rigidity as a rod in compensation for the reed of themselves. Such persons cannot be free, and they cannot tolerate freedom in others. These are the kinds of persons who tend to become totalitarians. We have been producing them in fairly large numbers in this country. We need to love each other more. We need to stimulate educators and awaken them to the full sense of their responsibility to make themselves acquainted with the latest findings of social biology, and to do something about applying them.

The possibilities for the development of co-operative human relations in this country are enormous. They need only be recognized and dealt with intelligently. We must recognize that the competive values of our culture put men in opposition to each other, and that under such conditions genuinely free inquiry is retarded. Under co-operative conditions, in which men have learned to share their interests and experiences, in which altruism rather than egoism is the dominant motive of behavior, freedom of inquiry is likely to be virtually unlimitedly encouraged and accelerated. This seems to me an ideal worth working for.

8. Time-Binding and the Concept of Culture

In June, 1921, an important book was published by an unknown author. The book was entitled *Manhood of Humanity,* and its author was Alfred Korzybski. By December, 1921, it had gone into its third printing, and in December, 1923, there was a fourth printing. Obviously quite a number of people found the book of interest, but who they were I cannot tell. Certain, it seems, the book did not cause much stir in the world or leave too deep an impression. I read this book for the first time in 1950 in its second posthumously published edition of June, 1950. It was only then that I learned that Korzybski's theory of time-binding had been developed long before the appearance of his *Science and Sanity* in 1933. It is to be hoped that with the re-publication of *Manhood of Humanity* that the book will, at last, come into its own, for it is perhaps more timely for our own day than it appears to have been for the time when it made its first appearance. For in *Manhood of Humanity* Korzybski attempted to lay the foundations for the science and art of what he then called by the new term "Human Engineering"—a term which has since been adopted by others, but not quite in the sense in which he meant it. Such a science, Korzybski pointed out, must be based upon a true understanding of the nature of man, upon what is essentially characteristic of him; and he endeavored to show that what distinguishes man from all other living things is his capacity for time-binding.

Before proceeding to the discussion of this brilliant conception, I must say a few words about the dangers of making one's appearance too early. Intellectually, Korzybski was a prematurely born child. The views set out in *Manhood of Humanity* appeared twenty-five to thirty years too soon. In 1921 Korzybski was occupied with science and its relation to ethics, with science and its relation to values, while his contemporaries in the sciences and in philosophy were denying that science or philosophy could provide a sound scientific foundation for leading the good life. We find Bertrand Russell, for example, writing, and Korzybski quotes this very passage: "The hope of satisfaction to our more human desires, the hope of demonstrating that the world has this or that ethical characteristic, is not one which, so far as I can see, philosophy can do anything whatever to satisfy." With this viewpoint Korzybski was entirely unable to agree, and I think, if we are to judge from his latest writings,[1] Russell would today be more inclined to agree with Korzybski's 1921 judgment than with his own of earlier years. Said Korzybski, in 1921:

[1] See Bertrand Russell, *The Impact of Science on Society*, Columbia University Press, New York, 1951.

The scientists, all of them, have their duties no doubt, but do not fully use their education if they do not try to broaden their sense of responsibility toward all mankind instead of closing themselves up in a narrow specialization where they find their pleasure. Neither engineers nor other scientific men have any right to prefer their own personal peace to the happiness of mankind; their place and their duty are in the front of struggling humanity, not in the unperturbed ranks of those who keep themselves aloof from life. If they are indifferent, or discouraged because they feel or think that they know that the situation is hopeless, it may be proved that undue pessimism is as dangerous a "religion" as any other blind creed.[2]

This was a view which was not popular when Korzybski wrote. Scientists were inclined to an ivory-towerism and a hand-washing indifference to the consequences of their work. Thirty years later scientists are pretty generally agreed that they must take a more responsible view of their place in the world. Korzybski's warning has come home to roost. "If those who know why and how neglect to act," he wrote in 1921, "those who do not know will act, and the world will continue to flounder."[3]

Korzybski was among the first to point out that "it is the great *disparity* between the rapid progress of the natural and technological sciences on the one hand and the slow progress of the metaphysical, so-called social sciences on the other hand, that sooner or later so disturbs the equilibrium of human affairs as to result periodically in those social cataclysms

[2] Alfred Korzybski, *Manhood of Humanity*, 2nd ed., Institute of General Semantics, Lakeville, Conn., 1950, p. 10.
[3] Ibid., p. 11.

which we call insurrections, revolutions and wars."[4] In the history of the development of the consciousness of this fact, Korzybski's name will come to occupy an honored place. When a society places its emphases on technology it produces a nation of technicians. Korzybski saw quite clearly where the emphasis must be placed if mankind is to survive—namely, upon the understanding of man's nature and the development of human relations on the basis of that understanding. The good life was what Korzybski was passionately interested in, and so he said, "Ethics is too fundamentally important a factor in civilization to depend upon a theological or a legal excuse; ethics must conform to the *natural* laws of human *nature*."[5] Korzybski clearly stated the consequences of "a system of social and economic order built exclusively on selfishness, greed, 'survival of the fittest,' and ruthless competition,"[6] and prescribed the remedy. The period of the *childhood* of humanity was one of arbitrary thought and confusion. "The period of humanity's *manhood* will," Korzybski wrote, "I doubt not, be a scientific period—a period that will witness the gradual extension of scientific method to all the interests of mankind—a period in which man will discover the essential nature of man and establish, at length, the science and art of directing human energies and human capacities to the advancement of human weal in accordance with the laws of human nature."[7]

[4] Ibid., p. 22.
[5] Ibid., pp. 34–35.
[6] Ibid., pp. 40–42.
[7] Ibid., pp. 44–45.

Korzybski died on March 1, 1950. Happily he lived to see his best hopes for the application of the scientific method to some of the interests of mankind get started, even though fitfully. The dangers of being born too early are largely personal. One suffers the pains of inappreciation for being ahead of one's time, and when the rest of mankind catches up, one has to have sense of humor enough to bear with equanimity the comment that after all there was nothing new in one's ideas, or that they were known all the time. Those who knew him can testify to the fact that Korzybski had a delightful sense of humor, so that neither the barking of the dogs of St. Ernulphus nor the patronizing gestures of the world of pernicious academia too much disturbed him.

In the present essay I wish to consider one of Korzybski's most significant contributions toward the better understanding of the nature of man, namely, his conception of time-binding.

Korzybski distinguished between the classes of life in the following manner: Since plants captured one kind of energy, converted it into another, and stored it up, he defined the plant class of life as the chemistry-binding class of life. Since animals were characterized by the freedom and faculty to move about in space, he defined animals as the space-binding class of life. He continues:

And now what shall we say of *human* beings? What is to be our definition of Man? Like the animals, human beings do indeed possess the *space-binding* capacity but, over and above that, human beings possess a most remarkable capacity which is entirely peculiar to them—I mean the capacity to summarize, digest, and appropriate the labors and experiences of the past; I mean the capacity to use the fruits of past labors and experiences as intellectual or spiritual capital for the developments in the present; I mean the capacity to employ as instruments of increasing power the accumulated achievements of the all-precious lives of the past generations spent in trial and error, trial and success; I mean the capacity of human beings to conduct their lives in the ever-increasing light of inherited wisdom; I mean the capacity in virtue of which man is at once the heritor of the by-gone ages and the trustee of posterity. And because humanity is just this magnificent natural agency by which the past lives in the present and the present for the future, I define HUMANITY, in the universal tongue of mathematics and mechanics, to be the TIME-BINDING CLASS OF LIFE.[8]

Very properly, Korzybski emphasized the importance of grasping the meaning of this definition of humanity as a starting point for discovering the natural laws of human nature—of the human class of life. Korzybski pointed out the immeasurable evils which have resulted from regarding man as a mere space-binder, an animal. In other words, Korzybski was from the first aware of the dangers of the biologistic fallacy or what I have elsewhere called "the pathetic fallacy," the belief that man is nothing but a function of his genes—a fallacy which many contemporary thinkers have even yet not succeeded in avoiding. Korzybski recognized that man was characterized by "properties of higher dimensionality," that everything which is really time-binding is in the human dimension.

Now, Korzybski's definition of humanity, of man, is virtually identical with the present-day anthro-

8 Ibid., pp. 59–60.

pologist's definition of culture. Here are some definitions of culture taken from the latest anthropological
works by leading anthropologists. Firth writes:

If society is taken to be an aggregate of social relations,
then culture is the content of those relations. Society
emphasizes the human component, the aggregate of people and relations between them. Culture emphasizes the
component of accumulated resources, immaterial as well
as material, which the people inherit, employ, transmute,
add to, and transmit. Having substance, if in part only
ideational, this component acts as a regulator to action.
From the behavioral aspect, culture is all learned behavior which has been socially acquired. It includes the
residual effects of social action. It is necessarily also an
incentive to action.[9]

Kluckhohn writes:

By "culture" anthropology means the total life way of
a people, the social legacy the individual acquires from
his group. Or culture can be regarded as that part of the
environment that is the creation of man . . . The general
abstract notion serves to remind us that we cannot explain acts solely in terms of the biological properties of
the people concerned, past experience, and the immediate situation. The past experience of other men in the
form of culture enters into almost every event.[10]

Herskovits writes:

Culture is the man-made part of the environment. Implicit in this is the recognition that man's life is lived in
a dual setting, the natural habitat and his social "en-

[9] Raymond Firth, *Elements of Social Organization,* Watts, London, 1951, p. 27.
[10] Clyde Kluckhohn, *Mirror for Man,* Whittlesey House, New
York, 1949, pp. 18–19.

vironment." The definition also implies that culture is more than a biological phenomenon. It includes all the elements in man's mature endowment that he has acquired from his group by conscious learning or, on a somewhat different level, by a conditioning process—techniques of various kinds, social and other institutions, beliefs, and patterned modes of conduct.[11]

White writes:

The physical category is composed of non-living phenomena or systems; the biological, of living organisms. The cultural category, or order, of phenomena is made up of events that are dependent upon a faculty peculiar to the human species, namely, the ability to use symbols. These events are the ideas, beliefs, languages, tools, utensils, customs, sentiments, and institutions that make up the civilization—or *culture,* to use the anthropological term—of any people, regardless of time, place, or degree of development. Culture is passed down from one generation to another, or, it may be borrowed freely by one tribe from another. Its elements interact with one another in accordance with principles of their own. Culture thus constitutes a supra-biological, or extra-somatic, class of events, a process *sui generis.*[12]

Compare with these definitions Korzybski's definition of culture, or civilization, in the 1921 *Manhood of Humanity.* Korzybski writes:

Civilization as a process is the process of binding time; progress is made by the fact that each generation adds to the material and spiritual wealth which it inherits. Past achievements—the fruit of bygone time—thus live in the

[11] Melville J. Herskovits, *Man and His Works,* Knopf, New York, 1948, pp. 17–18.
[12] Leslie A. White, *The Science of Culture,* Farrar, Straus, New York, 1949, pp. 15–16.

present, are augmented in the present, and transmitted to the future; the process goes on; time, the essential element, is so involved that, though it increases arithmetically, its fruit, civilization, advances, geometrically.[13]

The faculty peculiar to the human species, namely, the ability to make complex use of symbols, to which White refers, and upon which the development of the time-binding or cultural capacity of man is dependent was, of course, fully grasped by Korzybski, and here, too Korzybski was a forerunner of later thinkers in this field. Chapter IV of *Science and Sanity* is devoted to symbolism, and its very first words are: "The affairs of men are conducted by our own, man-made rules and according to man-made theories. Man's achievements rest upon the use of symbols. For this reason we must consider ourselves as a symbolic, semantic class of life, and those who rule the symbols, rule us."[14]

This viewpoint had already been worked out by the distinguished philosopher Ernst Cassirer in his *Philosophie der Symbolischen Formen,* published in three volumes in 1923–1929,[15] and in part made available in a new English version in the author's *An Essay on Man,* published in 1944.[16] In the latter work Cassirer writes:

Man has, as it were, discovered a new method of adapting himself to his environment. Between the receptor

13 Korzybski, *Manhood of Humanity,* p. 106.
14 Korzybski, *Science and Sanity,* 1st ed., Science Press, Lancaster, Pa., 1933, p. 76.
15 Bruno Cassirer, Berlin.
16 Yale University Press, New Haven; now available in complete English translation from the same press.

system and the effector system, which are to be found in all animal species, we find in man a third link which we may describe as the *symbolic system*. This new acquisition transforms the whole of human life. As compared with the other animals man lives not merely in a broader reality; he lives, so to speak in a new *dimension* of reality . . . Reason is a very inadequate term with which to comprehend the forms of man's cultural life in all their richness and variety. But all these forms are symbolic forms. Hence, instead of defining man as an *animal rationale*, we should define him as an *animal symbolicum*. By so doing we can designate his specific difference, and we can understand the new way open to man—the way to civilization.[17]

Writing at about the same time, and quite unbeknownst to each other, Korzybski and Cassirer had arrived at the same conclusions. Writing in 1944, Cassirer appears to have been quite unaware of Korzybski's work.

Sufficient, I hope, has been said to show that Korzybski's conception of time-binding and the anthropological conception of culture are virtually identical in character. It is rather sad to reflect that almost all anthropologists have overlooked this fact. It is to be hoped that this oversight will soon be remedied. Meanwhile, let us proceed now to discuss certain consequences which follow from the general theory of time-binding or culture for the development of a science of human nature and the science and art of human relations.

Korzybski pointed out that "human nature, this time-binding power, not only has the peculiar capa-

[17] Ernest Cassirer, *An Essay on Man*, Yale University Press, New Haven, 1944, pp. 24–26.

city for perpetual progress, but it has, over and above all animal propensities, certain qualities constituting it a distinctive dimension or type of life. Not only our whole collective life proves a love for higher ideals, but even our dead *give* us the rich heritage, material and spiritual, of all their toils. There is nothing mystical about it; to call SUCH a class a *naturally* selfish class is not only nonsensical but monstrous."[18] In this passage Korzybski comes very close to the discoveries which are only at this moment in process of being made concerning the nature of human nature. How right Korzybski was in referring to the belief in the class of humanity as naturally selfish as nonsensical and monstrous. The belief in the inherent selfishness of man, his innate naughtiness, inborn evil, aggressiveness and hostility, has taken many forms, and in each of its forms it has done untold personal and social damage. In the first place, that belief has conditioned our attitude toward our fellow men, and not only toward our fellow men, but toward those utterly defenseless, and dependent, potential time-binders, babies, infants, children, and adolescents. Our belief in the inherent naughtiness of man has caused us to make out of the process of child-rearing a discipline of restraints and frustrations, which has had the effect of seriously crippling and distorting most human beings who have been exposed to it. There is pretty good reason to believe that most of the personal and social tragedies which mankind has created and suffered from have been due to this erroneous belief and the consequences

[18] Korzybski, *Manhood of Humanity*, p. 143.

flowing from it as a result of the child-rearing processes it has conditioned. The belief in the innate
naughtiness of man is very old, but in the nineteenth
century it accrued unto itself a strong reinforcement
in the doctrine of "the survival of the fittest." "The
struggle for survival," "Nature red in tooth and
claw," "dog eat dog," and similar phrases were used
to describe the condition of animals in a state of
nature. Since man is an animal, it was argued, he has
inherited the same fundamental drives that keep the
rest of the animal kingdom going. Hence, man is by
nature aggressive and competitive, and, it was asked,
do we not see this in the evolution of human societies, and in the struggles of the classes in society?
The Spencerian application, known as Social Darwinism, of the theories of Darwin to the struggle for
survival in human societies further lent enchantment
to this particular view of the relations of men to one
another.

Searching for the inherent naughtiness and aggressiveness of the infant at birth and thereafter, contemporary investigators have been unsuccessful in
finding any evidences of it. The distinguished child
psychiatrist Dr. Lauretta Bender, having handled
thousands of children, writes from her great experience, in an important article entitled "The Genesis
of Hostility in Children," that far from being inborn, hostility or aggression in the child "is a symptom complex resulting from deprivations which are
caused by developmental discrepancies in the total
personality structure, such that the constructive patterned drives for action in the child find inadequate
means of satisfaction and result in amplification or

disorganization of the drives into hostile or destructive aggression." "The child," she writes, "acts as though there were an inherent awareness of his needs and there is thus the expectation of having them met. A failure in this regard is a deprivation and leads to frustration and a reactive aggressive response."

Indeed, the creativeness of the organism is directed toward maturation in terms of co-operation. Bender calls it "the inherent capacity or drive for normality." And she says, "The emphasis on the inborn or instinctive features of hostility, aggression, death wishes, and the negative emotional experience represents a one-sided approach which has led our students of child psychology astray."[19]

Maslow, in an article entitled "Our Maligned Animal Nature," writes, "I find children, up to the time they are spoiled and flattened out by the culture, nicer, better, more attractive human beings than their elders, even though they are of course more 'primitive' than their elders. The 'taming and transforming' that they undergo seem to hurt rather than help. It was not for nothing that a famous psychologist once defined adults as 'deteriorated children.' " "Could it be possible," Maslow inquires, "that what we need is a little *more* primitiveness and a little less *taming?*"[20]

Babies are born co-operative. What they want is to be co-operated with and to co-operate. When their needs for co-operation, for love, are frustrated, they

[19] Lauretta Bender, "Genesis of Hostility in Children," *American Journal of Psychiatry*, vol. 105, 1948, pp. 241–245.

[20] A. H. Maslow, "Our Maligned Animal Nature," *Journal of Psychology*, vol. 28, 1949, pp. 273–278.

may react with aggressive behavior. Aggressive behavior is originally a means of seeking and if possible compelling love. Aggression is practically always, if not always, the effect of love frustrated, or of the expectation of love frustrated. Children are not born selfish; they are made selfish by being forced to attend to their own needs as best they can through the failure of their discipliners to attend properly to children's needs for co-operation. The natural selfishness of the child is, indeed, a monstrous notion. It is an unfortunate projection by those who hold the notion of themselves upon the child. Man is not born evil—nor is he born neither good nor evil—but in a very positive sense he is born good, good in the sense of conferring survival benefits upon all with whom he comes into social relations. When one analyzes the basic needs of the human organism, those needs which must be satisfied if the organism is to survive, one finds that they are oriented in the direction of co-operation, of wanting to love, as well as wanting to be co-operated with and loved. It is in this sense that the organism may be said to be born good, and it is one of the few senses in which the word "good" means anything.[21]

Even if man had inherited any drives toward aggressiveness and combat by virtue of his capacity for time-binding, man would be capable of controlling the expression of such drives as to negate and completely nullify their potencies. As for the doctrine of

---

[21] See M. F. Ashley Montagu, *On Being Human*, Schuman, New York, 1950; *The Direction of Human Development*, Harper, New York, 1955.

"the survival of the fittest," Korzybski pointed out that this "in the commonly used animal sense is not a theory or principle for a 'time-binding' being .... its effect upon humanity is sinister and degrading."[22]

Thomas Henry Huxley, in a letter written October 27, 1890, wrote, "The unlucky substitution of 'survival of the fittest' for 'natural selection' has done much harm in consequence of the ambiguity of the 'fittest'—which many take to mean 'best' or 'highest'—whereas natural selection may work toward degradation *vide epizoa.*"[23]

What, ineed, is "fitness"? The Social Darwinists overlooked the fact that fitness is related to the current environment of a group, and without further scruple they converted "fittest" into "best." The current environment of man, perhaps more than at any time during his whole history, demands that he realize pretty rapidly in what his fitness must consist if he is to survive. As Korzybksi pointed out in 1921, "There is indeed a fine sense in which we can, if we choose, apply the expression—survival of the fittest— to the activity of the time-binding energies of man. Having the peculiar capacity to survive in our deeds, we have an inclination to use it and we survive in the deeds of our creation; and so there is brought about the 'survival of time' of higher and higher ideals ... It must be emphasized that the development of the higher ideals is due to the *natural* capacity of humanity; the impulse is simply a time-binding impulse."[24]

[22] Korzybski, *Manhood of Humanity*, p. 142.
[23] *Life and Letters of Thomas Henry Huxley*, Leonard Huxley, ed., D. Appleton, New York, 1901, vol. 2, p. 284.
[24] Korzybski, *Manhood of Humanity*, pp. 143–145.

Fitness for man, perhaps more than for any other creature, has fundamentally always consisted in and must increasingly come to consist in the subordination of individual competition to interpersonal co-operation, and of intergroup competition to co-operative association.[25] For this purpose it will be necessary to follow the highest ideals. But what are the highest ideals? Are they the same for all mankind? To answer the second question first, the ideals of human fitness are, indeed, the same for all mankind because these ideals are determined by the nature of human nature itself. As Korzybski stated, "Human logic ... the logic *natural* for man —will show us that 'good' and 'just' and 'right' are to have their significance defined and understood entirely in terms of human nature. Human nature—not animal nature—is to be the basis and guide of Human Enginering."[26]

Korzybski's contribution to the understanding of human nature did not lie in the fine analysis of its structure; his contribution lay in his distinguishing man from all other living creatures as the time-binder, and in emphasizing the fact that this capacity is a natural one. But unlike Thomas Henry Huxley, he saw that man doesn't have to struggle against his inner nature, but rather that he must realize it, for human nature, innate nature, was good *not* evil. And Korzybski held that the discovery of the highest ideals

[25] This is a précis of the words written by Patrick Geddes and and Arthur Thomson in their book *The Evolution of Sex*, Scott, London, 1889, p. 311: "Each of the greater steps in progress is in fact associated with an increased measure of subordination of individual competition to reproductive or social ends, and of inter-specific competition to cooperative association."

[26] Korzybski, *Manhood of Humanity*, p. 149.

should be based on the scientific understanding of
the nature of human nature, in other words, that
"what is right is what is right for human nature." I
believe that when everything is said and done this
assertion will be found to represent the fundamental
formula for the life of man, that what is right is what
is right for human nature. To some of us who are
working in this field it is already evident that this is,
indeed, so. For the findings of modern workers have
shown unequivocally that insofar as men depart from
the biologic demands of their innate nature, they fall
ill and become disoperative, and that insofar as they
conform to the requirements of their nature, they
function harmoniously and well. But in order to recognize this fact it is first necessary to understand the
nature of human nature. This is an area in which the
most significant work has been done in the twentieth
century, and in which a tremendous amount of work
remains to be done before we can really speak of
understanding the nature of human nature, but for
some who have been interested in putting together
the findings of modern science on the nature of human nature, the general picture is clear, and it is in
complete conformity with Korzybski's views. In the
space remaining I propose to give an outline of that
general picture.

Man is, of course, part of the world of nature. He
comes into being in fundamentally the same way as
all other creatures, that is, by reproduction. The reproductive process is the fundamental social process,
and it is this reproductive process which determines
the pattern of man's, as well as of all other living
creatures, biologic life. The process of reproduction

is an interdependent-dependent one, and that is the essence of the biologic relation between organisms, interdependency and dependency. This holds true whether we are concerned with unicellular or multicellular organisms, for the amoeba and for man. Man, however, is perhaps more strikingly characterized by this interdependency-dependency trait than any other living creature. Following conception he spends nine months in that dependent-interdependent state, and after birth he continues to spend several years in dependent-interdependent relationship of the most dependent kind with other human beings. Dependency is man's basic biologic state and interdependency is man's social state. Man comes into the world biologically wanting to be dependent and interdependent. How do we know this for a fact? We know this for a fact because if the interdependency needs of the potentially human organism are not satisfied, the organism simply does not develop as a human being, and if its dependency needs are not satisfied, it can develop only in a crippled sort of way. The infant's drives are oriented in the direction of love and co-operation. It wants to love and it wants to be co-operated with, and if it is loved and co-operated with, then it develops in every way more efficiently as a loving, co-operative human being, and also as a healthy physical organism. How do we know these things for facts? We know these things for facts because if the potentially human organism is not adequately loved or co-operated with it fails to develop as an adequate human being, as a being who is functioning harmoniously and who is adequately capable of loving and co-operating with others. The evidence for these relationships has recently been ably discussed and summarized in a World Health Organization publication entitled *Maternal Care and Mental Health* and written by the English psychiatrist John Bowlby.[27] As for the relation between adequate love in infancy and proper physical growth and development, the work of Dr. Ralph Fried at Cleveland[28] and of others elsewhere is conclusive. This should not surprise us in the least, for the organism is a whole, and one cannot deprive it of necessary stimulations in any part of it without affecting the whole organism—that is what the word "organism," properly understood, in part implies. Not only this, we now know that when children within the first year and during the greater part of their first six years are adequately loved, they are likely to grow up to be adequately loving and co-operative, healthy persons, persons who are capable of taking the stresses and strains of life very much more efficiently than those who have not been adequately loved during their first half-dozen years.[29] From studies which have been made among the nonliterate peoples of the world, the so-called "primitive peoples," anthropologists have found that the way in which children are brought up is closely related to their personality structure, and on

[27] Issued in the United States by Columbia University Press, New York, 1951.

[28] Ralph Fried and M. F. Mayer, "Socio-Emotional Factors Accounting for Growth Failure of Children Living in an Institution," *Journal of Pediatrics*, vol. 33, 1948, pp. 444–456. See also Harold G. Wolff, et al., eds., *Life Stress and Bodily Disease*, Williams & Wilkins, Baltimore, 1950; Hans Selye, *The Stress of Life*, McGraw-Hill, New York, 1956.

[29] See James L. Halliday, *Psychosocial Medicine*, Norton, New York, 1948.

the whole, the conclusion is that the more adequately children have been loved during their first six years, the more loving they usually are as adults, while the more frustrated children have been during their first six years, the more frustrated they are as adult personalities and the more unloving. This may be putting the essence of the findings in an oversimplified form, but I don't know of any better way of stating the facts in a few words than in this manner.

What, in brief, has been discovered is that to live as if to live and love were one is the only way of life for human beings, because, indeed, this is the way of life which the innate nature of man demands. The highest ideals of man, therefore, spring from man's own nature, and the highest of these ideals and the one which must inform all others is *love*. This is not a new discovery in the world; what is new is that scientists should have made it by scientific means. What contemporary scientists working in this field have done is to give, without in most cases being aware of it or intending to, a scientific validation to the Sermon on the Mount—love thy neighbor as thyself, do unto others as you would have them do unto you—principles which were enunciated by many philosophers, prophets, and seers, long before the birth of Jesus. Indeed, every people has at some time or another arrived at this elementary piece of wisdom on the basis of experience, and most peoples have, more or less successfully, attempted to live by these principles because they have discovered them to be the most efficient by which to live. This, at any rate, is their theory enshrined in their religious and civil codes, but the practice seems to lag far behind the

religious theory and the civil codes so frequently derived from and based on those religious theories.
What is the reason for the difference between theory
and practice?

In the light of our modern studies the answer to
this question would not seem to be a very difficult
one, although any answer that is returned is likely to
be an oversimplification. The reason why people
don't live by the principle of love is that they haven't
been raised by it. On the other hand, most of them
have been raised by the principle of systematic frustration—which in our culture we often call "discipline." Most of the so-called civilized world simply
hasn't loved little children adequately enough, no
matter what their holy books have said about love,
and if you've been pushed around as a child you are
likely to grow up as a pusher-around of others when
you are an adult. You can be terribly interested in
love if you've been deprived of it as a child, but you
will be unable adequately to receive it and unable to
give it. Children may be told that they are being
loved while at the same time they are being frustrated. What they remember is the frustration, not
the love. No matter what parents say they believe,
children believe that parents believe what they do,
not what they say.

How, then, is one to escape from this vicious circle
of frustrated children growing up into frustrating
parents who in turn produce frustrated children who
grow up to be frustrated parents? The answer is: By
educating the world of human beings in the facts, by
showing all who are capable of learning it what the

true nature of human nature is and why it must be respected, what it is that human nature demands and why those demands must be obeyed. As Bacon put it, "Nature to be commanded must be obeyed." We must teach, all who are capable of learning—and everyone is capable of learning—what happens when one doesn't obey the innate demands of one's being, and what happens when one does. We must, in short, teach the art and science of human nature, the art and science of human relations. We must relieve mankind of the load of myths which has been weighing it down for so long about the nature of Nature and the nature of human nature. We must disabuse humanity of the myth of the inherent naughtiness of mankind and present the facts which will permit men to judge for themselves what the truth really is. This can be achieved by many different approaches and at innumerable different levels, but the one method in which I place the greatest faith is education. Education must be conceived as bringing out the best that is within each person by making available to him all the encouragements and supports and stimulations which he requires, in order to enable him to become a loving, co-operative, nonconflictful person. A person so educated will not only be aware of what is right with the world but also what is wrong with it, and he will be equipped with both the knowledge and the desire necessary to improve it nearer that ideal of what it should and can be. A person so educated will not be a competitor, but a co-operator, a person for whom altruism will be passion and selfishness a disorder, a person wise enough to know that

> He who would love his fellow men
> Must not expect too much of them.

A person so educated will want to improve the world as he finds it, not accepting things as they are, but having the wisdom to know what things to accept and what to change. He will not risk wrecking the social machinery by exceeding the speed limit of rational inquiry; he will not abolish anything but merely make it necessary to discontinue it, dispelling fear by supplying facts and knowledge. A person so educated will recognize the strange necessity of beauty, will have a sense of personal responsibility for decency and justice, will never burn the smoke of incense before an empty shrine. A person, in short, who having had a loving order made within himself, will make loving order in the world,

> . . . be to other souls
> The cup of strength in some great agony,
> Enkindle generous ardour, feed pure love,
> Beget the smiles that have no cruelty,
> Be the sweet presence of a good diffused,
> And in diffusion ever more intense!
>   —GEORGE ELIOT

May I conclude with some words from Korzybski's 1921 *Manhood of Humanity*:

In humanity's manhood, patriotism—the love of country—will not perish—far from it—it will grow to embrace the world. Your "state" and mine will be the Human State—a Cooperative Commonwealth of Man—a democracy in fact and not merely in name. It will be a natural organic embodiment of the civilizing energies—the wealth-producing energies—characteristic of the human class of life. Its larger affairs will be guided by the science and art of Human Engineering—not by ignorant and grafting "politicians"—but by scientific men, by honest men who *know*.

Is it a *dream?* It *is* a dream, but the dream will come true. It is a scientific dream and science will make it a living reality.[30]

[30] Korzybski, *Manhood of Humanity*, pp. 199–200.

9. Man—And Human Nature

Ideas taught do not have greater power
than they receive from those who are taught.

—FRANCESCO SANCHEZ (1552-1632)
Quod Nihil Scitur

What is man? What is human nature? These are questions which have exercised the speculative faculty of human beings ever since they became capable of self-reflection. As we examine the cultures of humanity, that is to say, the man-made parts of the human environment, or as Sir John Myres [1][1] has put it, what remains of men's past working on their present to shape their future, we find that the answers to these questions are usually interrelated in a special way. We find that the answer to the question, What is man? is usually returned in terms of what man's nature is conceived to be.

In other words, we at once perceive that most cultures begin with a particular conception of human nature and then proceed to fashion their man according to it. Man is custom-made, tailored according to the pattern prevailing in his particular culture. And

[1] The figures in brackets refer to the bibliography on pp. 147–149.

as students of human society have shown, man's societies are remarkably various. Within the great range of human cultures the views held concerning the nature of man are probably as numerous as the leaves in Vallombrosa. In point of fact, we know astonishingly little of the views concerning the nature of man held by nonliterate peoples. In most cases we know more about what they think of their supernaturals than we do about what they think of the nature of man [2]. But we do know a little, and together with what we have learned of the views of man held by the literate cultures of the world, we can say that these well-nigh exhaust the envisageable possibilities. A comparative study of the "man-views," as they may be called, has never been made. It would be most revealing. The nearest thing that we have to it at the present time are the studies in culture and personality that anthropologists have initiated in recent years. Such studies, in which the attention is largely focused on child-rearing practices and their relation to the development of personality, throw considerable light upon the man-views of different cultures and represent perhaps the best means available to us of discovering the nature of those views [3].

For the cultures of the Western world the work of psychoanalytically oriented investigators has proven equally illuminating. There has been not merely a convergence of interest but an increasingly active and fruitful partnership between anthropologists and psychiatrists [4]. There is every promise that this collaboration will grow and increase, and also that it will have the most beneficial effects upon the social and medical sciences to the great advantage of humanity. I am convinced that the healthy course upon which we are now embarked will lead to the discovery that medicine is possibly more of a social science than it is by many at present allowed to be [5].

I should like to consider with you the conceptions of man and of human nature which prevail in the Western world. There are several reasons why at this time we should pause to examine critically the beliefs held in the Western world respecting man and his nature.

In the first place, it is a good practice, from time to time, to hang a question mark on the beliefs we take most for granted, for those beliefs may in fact be wholly or partly erroneous. Many of our most entrenched beliefs, when subjected to such questioning, are found to be so encrusted with age and fortified by rationalization that they have become impervious to any but the most critical examination. In the second place, such beliefs may be very damaging without our being aware of the fact. In the third place, while it is seldom possible to trace the origins of many cultural traditions, it *is* possible to trace something of the complex history of the man-view so widely held throughout the Western world, and hence, if we are in error, we may yet learn something of the route by which we arrived at what may be described as our compulsive enslavement to destructive certainties—on the very edge of doom. In the fourth place, as a consequence of the labors of many workers in the medical, psychiatric, social, and biological fields, a great deal of largely unintegrated knowledge has been accumulated which renders a revaluation of our traditional man-view urgently necessary.

By "traditional" is to be understood not only the beliefs that we have inherited from antiquity, but also those of more recent vintage which have contributed in any way to the traditional complex of beliefs.

Can we give a brief statement which fairly represents the essence of this traditional complex of beliefs?

A very short statement would be that in the Western world it is generally believed man is a "cussed" and "ornery" creature. There is good and evil in him, but the good is so shot through with the evil, that one must constantly be policing the evil, in order to give the good an opportunity to express itself. Child-rearing practices, education, religion, indeed most, if not all, of man's major social institutions testify to the persuasiveness of this view of human nature.

Most of the trouble in which man finds himself is held to be due to his inherent brattishness, hence the necessity of designing social controls calculated to keep the brute in him in check, so that the amount of trouble into which he gets is kept to more or less manageable proportions [6].

How old is this view in the Western tradition? It seems to be as old as the oldest traceable traditions of the West. These traditions were largely reinforced and supplemented in the West by the introduction of Christianity and the teachings of the Old and New Testaments, plus the addition of Greek pessimism—the Hebraeo-Christian-Greek tradition. By "the He-

braeo-Christian-Greek tradition" I mean principally
the interpretation given to the teachings of Jesus by
a member of the Greek culture-world. This member
was the divinely obsessed, Jesus-intoxicated, uncom-
promising zealot, Saul called Paul. It is to St. Paul
rather than to Jesus that Christianity owes its basic
form and much of its content. It is to St. Paul that
the Western world is indebted for the peculiar development of the doctrine of Original Sin and the
inherent wickedness of man—a dogma, so far as we
know, not even remotely suggested by anything Jesus
ever said or did.[2]

St. Paul's teachings were systematically elaborated
by the Church Fathers, so that they became accepted
doctrine throughout the length and breadth of Chris-
tendom. Jansenism and Puritanism are two, by no
means extreme, forms of this doctrine, the one hold-
ing that man becomes progressively more evil as he
lives, and the other that the proof of man's inherent
evil nature lies in his apparently unlimited capacity
for enjoyment. For Jonathan Edwards (1703–1758),
for example, "In Adam's fall We sinned all," and
from the consequences of this sin there was no escape
except by virtue of divine grace [7].

Hannah More (1745–1833), the English bluestock-
ing, praises the dictum that children should be
taught that they are "naturally depraved creatures,"
and goes on to add that a stroll in the public gardens

[2] The doctrine of Original Sin, in its various forms, enshrines
the belief that the sin of Adam "was the sin of Human nature
(Rom. v. 12–21) and inheres as habitual sin in all who share in
that nature by bodily generation." Donald Attwater, ed., *A Cath-
olic Dictionary*, Macmillan, New York, 1941, p. 490.

on Sunday evening or attendance at a sacred concert are to be condemned as sinful [8].

As Muller has remarked, "Throughout Christian history the conviction that man's birthright is sin has encouraged an unrealistic acceptance of remediable social evils, or even a callousness about human suffering. It helps to explain the easy acceptance of slavery and serfdom, and a record of religious atrocity unmatched by any other high religion" [9].

> Have two thousand years of saying mass
> Gone as far as poison gas?
> Or taken us further, with aplomb,
> To genuflect before the atom bomb?

To explain the existence of evil, the common appeal of many early peoples has been to a "Fall" from a prior state of perfection. Nothing could be more natural than such an explanation. It is found in early Chaldean legends. Hesiod (*Works and Days*, lines 109–201) tells how "the golden race . . . as gods were wont to live." Then, Pandora ensnared her husband Epimetheus, in disobedience of the divine command, to open the box with which she had been presented by the gods, whereupon trouble and sorrow escaped into the world, mitigated only by hope.

The early and widespread beliefs in "the Fall," in doctrines of inherent natural depravity or the original sinfulness of human nature, have enjoyed so wide an appeal, we may suspect, because they have served to shift the responsibility for man's evil behavior from himself to his inherent nature. As a self he can strive to be good, but always in the presence of the dangerous undertow of his evil and destructive impulses, which are constantly threatening to pull him under.

The secular experience of humanity during the last two thousand years, the internecine wars, the bloodshed, plunder and treachery, the general inhumanity of man to man, has in almost every way served to confirm the Church Fathers' view of the natural depravity of man.

The "nasty brute" view of man which was developed by Thomas Hobbes (1588–1679) in *Leviathan* (1651) stated the rationalist viewpoint very clearly. Man, argued Hobbes, is simply the motions of the organism, and man is by nature a selfishly individualistic animal at constant war with all other men [10]. Except for the eighteenth-century Enlightenment interlude, this view of man's nature has enjoyed uninterrupted sovereignty up to the present day. What is more, it has received the validation of two separate scientific disciplines, namely Darwinian evolutionary theory and Freudian psychology.

Life in the state of nature, the Darwinians convincingly showed, is a struggle for existence, characterized by ruthless competition. Conflict and combat is the rule, indeed, the law of nature. In the social-economic context of the day, the survival of the fittest was taken to mean the survival of the fightingest (or anyone with an income of over $2,500 per annum). The weakest went to the wall and the strongest took all the prizes. Nature was "red in tooth and claw," and though it shrieked against the creed of man, man was still a part and a product of nature [11].

In a famous article, published in February, 1888, which became known as "the Struggle for Life Manifesto," Thomas Henry Huxley put the viewpoint he so ably represented in these forceful words: "From the point of view of the moralist, the animal world is on about the same level as a gladiator's show. The creatures are fairly well treated, and set to fight—whereby the strongest, the swiftest and the cunningest live to fight another day. The spectator has no need to turn his thumbs down, as no quarter is given" [12]. Numberless such statements could be cited from the authorities of the day. In our own time a world-famous anthropologist, and one of the kindliest of men, Sir Arthur Keith (1866–1955) could remark, "Nature keeps her orchard healthy by pruning; war is her pruning-hook. We cannot dispense with her services. This harsh and repugnant forecast of man's future is wrung from me. The future of my dreams is a warless world" [13].

Students of the human mind have been no less influenced by Darwinian theory than students of the evolution of the human body. Any competent comparative anatomist could demonstrate the evidences of structures long useless in man but quite functional in his ancestors, and, of course, most of man's anatomical characters he held in common with his nearest living relatives, the great apes. It was to be expected, then, that his psychological endowment would also exhibit some persisting evidences of his lowly origins.

It was true that man was something more than a beast, yet it was equally true that he was not less than a beast, that he was still in part beast, and in spite of such humanity as he was capable of achieving, it was only too evident that the beast in him would keep on creeping out. This viewpoint is still widely held at the present time—whether the beastliness is of the Passionate Pauline or of the Dismal Darwinist variety.

This general viewpoint has received what is perhaps its most striking reinforcement from a source which undoubtedly represents the most perceptive contribution to our understanding of human nature in the history of humanity. I refer to the psychoanalytic theories of Sigmund Freud (1856–1939).

Freud was born three years before the publication of Darwin's *Origin of Species*. Freud grew up in the Darwinian age, and was himself a thoroughgoing Darwinist. He was a product of the Hebraeo-Christian tradition, of the period of Franz Josef and the Victorian age, the chief concern of which was the preoccupation with morality, in which the two elemental forces of Love and Death fought with each other for supremacy. It was not surprising that Freud was unable to avoid structuring what he perceived of the dynamics of the human mind in terms of the dynamics of the human society with which he was familiar, precisely as the Darwinians were unable to avoid seeing nature in terms of the competitive struggle for existence which prevailed in nineteenth-century England. There is nothing new in the discovery that we tend to see the world according to the kingdom that is within us, and the kingdom that is within us is likely to be the one in which we have been socialized.

Freud, as you know, conceived of the mental life

of man as the expression principally of the reciprocal interplay of two basic instincts, the one Eros or Love, and the other Thanatos or Death. What began, as Freud himself put it, as a speculative "often far-fetched idea" [14] terminated in Freud's final work [15] as an article of faith. Exploring the "idea out of curiosity to see whither it will lead," [14] Freud became so enamored of the death instinct that thereafter he was unable to resist the tendency to see death and destruction wherever he could. This proceeded to such an extent in Freud that he was unable to see the answer to the question which he said "we do not know how to answer, and therefore we should feel relieved if the whole structure of our arguments were to prove erroneous. The opposition of ego- (or death) instincts and sexual (life-) instincts would then disappear, and the repetition-compulsion would also lose the significance we have attributed to it" [16].

The question is again stated in Freud's last published work, *An Outline of Psychoanalysis.* He writes, "If we suppose that living things appeared later than inanimate ones and arose out of them, then the death instinct agrees with the formula that we have stated, to the effect that instincts tend toward a return to an earlier state . We are unable to apply the formula to Eros (the love instinct). That would be to imply that living substance had once been a unity but had subsequently been torn apart and was now tending toward re-union" [15].

In a matrix of divisiveness, death, and destruction, it is understandable why Freud should have failed to see the answer—which almost any elementary student of biology could have given him—to the question he asked. Freud here presents a striking illustration of the dangers which arise from becoming too enamored with theory, namely, the resulting insensibility to facts.

Of course living substance had once been a unity, and we see this unity at a complex level in the single cell; the tearing apart is seen in the process of fission, in the one cell coming into being from the other, and the "tending toward re-union," we see not merely in the conjugal behavior of organisms but in the innate tendency of one organism or cell to react in a definite manner with another organism or cell— a process which has been called *prototaxis* [17].

Organisms are environmental necessities of each other. The fact that all living organisms tend to form social aggregates, that is, to interact with each other in a mutually beneficial manner, is proof of the deep-seated nature of this universal drive. I have elsewhere suggested that *the fundamentally social nature of all living things has its origin in the reproductive relationship between genitor and offspring,* in the fact that the life of either one or the other is at some time dependent upon the potential or actual being of the other, and that the social relationships existing between organisms up to and including man represent the largely unconscious development of the interdependent relationship between mother and child as experienced in the reproductive state [18].

Reproduction, in sexual forms, is a result of sexual union. The tendency of life is not to destroy itself but to reproduce and maintain itself. Sexual conjugation and reproduction are related not simply as

cause and effect, in that order, but conjugation occurs as an effect of reproduction. The "repetition-
compulsion" of which Freud speaks, the desire to
return to the unitary state, the drive toward union,
arises out of the fact that all living things originate
out of other living things. The drive to be together
is an expression of the desire to be united with one's
kind, to be unified without being reduced to uniformity.

I wish to suggest here that in our tradition, from
the earliest times up to the present day, the basic
assumption concerning the nature of human nature,
namely, that it is either wholly or partially evil, in
reality represents the error of mistaking the effect for
the cause. The evidence indicates that the evil in
man is not the cause of his behavior but the effect
of the behavior of others upon him.

I know of no evidence, which will withstand critical examination, that any human being is born with
the slightest element of evil within him, whether
that evil be called original sin or a drive or tendency
to destruction. If there is anyone anywhere who can
produce such evidence I challenge him to do so. I
don't think that it can be produced.

The tradition of inherent human depravity is an
unsound one, and it is one that has been extremely
damaging in its human and social effects. The day
is, perhaps, not far removed when humanity will
look back upon its "unregenerate" view of itself as
a perverse phase of its development during what may
be called its trial-and-error period. The first million
years, it would seem, are the hardest. We shall do
well to recall that in the continuum of life man as

a species is but a flash in the pan, the most recent of
nature's experiments, a creature that, with somewhat
oafish arrogance, has so prematurely named itself
Homo sapiens, when the more appropriate appela-
tion at the present time would be *Homo sap,* with
the *-iens* to be added when it has been earned. Humanity is in the childhood of its development—it
has yet to achieve maturity. Man, a mutational accident, has inherited great riches which he has not yet
learned to use. Nature's most favored child, he be-
haves like a spoiled brat. He has to learn to grow up.
Will he succeed?

That human beings possess the potentialities for
great wisdom is admitted, even by those who, in the
searing light of the hydrogen bomb, have concluded
that the goose is cooked—or is it vaporized? As a
matter of pure, practical common sense, I should
think that the only philosophically tenable position
for a pessimist, these days, is optimism.

Freud, as you know, certainly entertained grave
doubts as to man's future. Toward the end of his
life he grew more pessimistic than ever. In *Civilization and Its Discontents* Freud speaks almost literally
in the words of Thomas Hobbes. He says:

. . . men are not gentle, friendly creatures wishing for
love . . . but . . . a powerful measure of desire for aggression has to be reckoned as part of their instinctual
endowment . . . *Homo homini lupus;* who has the courage to dispute it in the face of all the evidence in his
own life and in history? This aggressive cruelty usually
lies in wait for some provocation, or else it steps into
service of some other purpose, the aim of which might
as well have been achieved by milder measures. In cir-

cumstances that favor it, when those forces in the mind which ordinarily inhibit it cease to operate, it also manifests itself spontaneously and reveals men as savage beasts to whom the thought of sparing their own kind is alien. Anyone who calls to mind the atrocities of the early migrations, of the invasion by the Huns or by the so-called Mongols under Jenghiz Khan and Tamurlane, of the sack of Jerusalem by the pious Crusaders, even indeed the horrors of the last world-war, will have to bow his head humbly before the truth of this view of man. [19]

It is, perhaps, not unfair to say that the view of man here enshrined by Freud has had a powerful influence upon both psychiatric theory and practice. And this view of man has served, of course, to give the final validation to the traditional conception of human nature.

What can we do other than humbly bow our heads, as Freud suggests, to the "truth" of this so frequently reinforced tradition concerning the innate aggressiveness of man? I would suggest that while the scientific attitude should embrace a certain amount of humility it is by no means a part of that attitude to bow one's head even in the face of the so-called facts, for a fact is at best little more than an interpretation, the consensus of opinion of those who *should* know. Only too often facts, and even laws of nature, turn out to be nothing but theories which have been smuggled across the border without benefit of the proper scientific customs examination of their right to enter the realm of fact. The proper attitude in the face of facts or theories is not belief or disbelief, but dispassionate inquiry.

Freud expressed the belief of the greater part of

Western tradition when he wrote that "men are not gentle, friendly creatures wishing for love," but that they have a "constitutional tendency to aggression against one another." The question we have to ask is: What is the evidence for these statements?

The answer we are given is: The behavior of human beings. Human beings are hostile to one another; they hate, betray, destroy, kill, and murder. The human record, it is alleged, provides a ghastly record of man's constitutional aggressiveness.

Let us examine these allegations. It is beyond dispute that the human record provides abundant proof of human aggressiveness. But what that record does not provide is proof of its innateness. And here it may be pointed out that when Freud uses the word "constitutional" he uses it incorrectly, as many others have done before and since, as if it were equivalent to "innate." Whereas the fact is that "constitution" represents the realization of the organism as an expression of the interaction between its genetic endowment and the environment. Similarly, heredity does not consist only of genetic endowment, but of genetic endowment as developed under the modifying influence of the environment. What the organism inherits is a genetic endowment *and* an environment.

The genetic endowment of man is unique, for it represents the most plastic system of potentialities for developing capacities which we recognize as uniquely human. These capacities in essence may be summed up in one word, namely, *educability*. Educability is, indeed, *the* species character of man. The evidence is quite clear that everything we know and do *as human beings* we have had to learn, which means that we have had to be consciously or uncon-sciously taught by other human beings.

Man is not born with a built-in system of responses to the environment as are most other creatures. On the other hand, man is born with a built-in system of malleable potentialities which under environmental stimulation are capable of being caused to respond in a large variety of ways.

What we have traditionally understood as human nature, and what we understand human nature to be to this day, is not our genetic endowment, which may be called *primary potential human nature,* but the expression of the potentialities constituting that en-dowment under the influence of the human environ-ment, that is, *secondary human nature.* It is second-ary human nature that we know as *human nature,* and this human nature is not built in but is en-culturated into us. Primary human nature we see overtly in the early infant's expression of the basic needs—and generally we see in them only what we are prepared to see.

Is there a basic need for aggression? Is there such a thing as an aggressive drive? Has anyone ever ob-served "aggressive instincts," as Freud calls them, in human beings or the "love of aggression in individu-als" as an expression of primary nature? I know of no one who has done so, for "the tendency to agres-sion" and the "love of aggression" of which Freud and others speak is not observable at any time in any human being who has not secondarily acquired it.

A distinguished psychiatrist, in a widely read book, has poured scorn upon "sociologists, anthropologists, and others whose psychological ground work is relatively deficient" for regarding aggressiveness as "the result of 'the culture' in which the individual lives. They make," he says, "such nonsensical propositions as that all aggression is the result of frustration. Anyone who has had his toe stepped on, which is certainly not a frustration, knows how inadequate such a formula is. Furthermore," he adds, "it [we are not sure here whether the "it" refers to the "formula" or to the sociologists and anthropologists] completely ignores the question of where the aggressive energy comes from which is provoked by the frustration, and this is what the instinct theory attempts to answer" [20].

It is an excellent rule not to step on anyone's toes, for what I had thought were obvious reasons. I shall do my best not to do so. But it seems to me, if I may mix a mataphor, that the writer has, as it were, fallen into his own trap. He denies that aggressiveness is "the result of the culture,'" and he calls "nonsensical" the proposition that all aggression is the result of frustration. Yet the fact is that the relation of culture to the determinants of behavioral response could not be better illustrated than by this example of toe-stepping. For when a person living in a so-called primitive culture steps on the toes of another, he is likely to do so with bare feet and is thus unlikely to hurt or frustrate the other, and there will be no aggressive behavior. Whereas in a culture in which one wears shoes, one is likely to hurt and frustrate the person upon whose toe one has stepped —but whether one will elicit aggressiveness or not will depend upon the manner in which the stepped-upon has learned to respond to his frustrations.[3] If we accept the generally accepted definition of a frustration as the thwarting of an expected satisfaction, then it may perhaps be acknowledged that having one's toe stepped on may be experienced as a frustration of the expectation of the enjoyment of pursuing, in the words of Thomas Gray:

> . . . the noiseless tenor of [one's] way.
> Yet e'en these bones from insult to protect . . .

We need not go further than our own culture to observe how the response to frustration is bred (in the sense of being trained) into one—and is therefore culturally determined. An ill-bred person may react to having his toes stepped on with aggressive behavior, a well-bred person may react with nonaggressive behavior. But this may reflect no more than a difference in the learned ability to control the expression of aggression. On the other hand, the different responses may actually represent a difference in feeling content—in the one case aggressive feeling being present and in the other not present.

Other things being equal, we can take this difference in feeling to be an expression of a nervous system that has been socialized in different ways in connection with the frequency of frustration and the training in the kind of responses permitted. I have not the least doubt that different cultures produce

[3] I recall here the definitions of a student of mine. She wrote: "A mentally healthy person is one who has learned to live with his frustrations in a satisfactory sort of way. A neurotic is one who has learned to live with his frustrations in an unsatisfactory sort of way."

differently organized nervous systems. The evidence from different cultures of the manner in which response to frustration is trained is most impressive. Anthropologists have made the accounts of these differences so widely available that thousands of readers now know that the Zuñi Indians avoid every form of aggressive behavior, that the expression of behavior is highly institutionalized among the Kwakiutl of the Northwest Pacific Coast, that the Dobuans of the Western Pacific are pathologically aggressive, and that the Arapesh of New Guinea control some forms of aggression but not others.

Where does all the aggressive energy come from which is provoked by frustration? This question is, indeed, a puzzler, for it certainly does not emanate from the store of aggressiveness which man has inherited from his animal ancestors. If we are to judge from man's closest living relatives, the chimpanzee and the gorilla, man is descended from among the least aggressive creatures in the animal kingdom. Under natural conditions these creatures are completely peaceful, vegetarian, and will not hurt so much as a fly. It is our own ferocity that we have projected upon these gentle creatures. And we have conceived of nature in much the same way, having made of it, in our mind's eye, what we have made of the world of man. We are the only species that makes war on its own kind, yet we speak of "the war of nature." But nature does not make war on itself—only certain branches of mankind do. Warlike activities at the present day are unknown to many human groups. All the evidence indicates that war was a very late development in the history of man, not appearing until the Neolithic, some ten thousand years ago [21].

Where, then, does the aggressive energy of human beings come from if not from the stores of the "far-fetched" notion of a death instinct? From all the available evidence it seems to me that the answer is unequivocally clear: The so-called aggressive energy of human beings comes from the same source as that which supplies the energy to love. And what is that source? It is the total energy system of the organism, an energy system which is directed toward the achievement of living in growth and development—the birthright of every living thing. The directiveness of the organism's activities is toward life, *not* toward death.

The energy subserving the functions of love is no different from that which supplies the dynamos of aggression. The one is not a transformation of the other; it is the same energy used to achieve the same ends—the maintenance and growth of the self. Aggression *is* love—it is love frustrated. This is the relationship to which, as a student of human nature, I see all the evidence pointing. In *The Origins of Love and Hate,* a work which I regard as the most original and helpfully constructive critique of Freud in existence, Ian Suttie describes aggression as a technique or mode for compelling the attention which one has been denied. Hate, Suttie points out, is not a primal independent instinct, but a development or intensification of separation-anxiety which in turn is evoked by a threat against love. Hate "is the maximal ultimate appeal in the child's power—the most difficult for the adult to ignore. Its purpose is not death-seeking or death-dealing, but the preservation of the self from the isolation which is death, and the restoration of a love relationship" [22].

Since those words were published, twenty years ago, much confirmation has been brought to them by the researches of such workers as Lowrey [23], Levy [24], Goldfarb [25], Bender [26], Spitz [27], Bowlby [28], Banham [29], Maslow [30], and many others [31]. These and other relevant researches prove that the child is dependent for its healthy development upon the love that it is given, and what is quite as important, the love that it is able to give to others. From the moment of birth on, the infant seeks to re-establish its connection with the mother. Just as the fertilized ovum seeks to attach itself to the womb, so the newborn seeks to attach itself to the mother, and in relation to her to realize its further development—a development which is a continuation of that begun in the womb. From the first, mother and child are in a symbiotic relationship in which they confer mutually advantageous benefits upon each other. The child is as necessary for the parents further development as is the mother for the child's development. And the directiveness of the child's behavior is toward loving others. The child's need for love from others is important principally because that love is the most significant developer of its own capacity to love others.

Indeed, it may unequivocally be stated that every human being is born *good*, good in the sense that every infant is born with all its energies oriented in the direction of conferring and receiving, of exchanging, creatively enlarging benefits. The purposes of the infant are constructive—*not* destructive. He desires to live as if to live and love were one.

When the stimulations necessary for the development of his need to love and be loved are withheld, we know that the child will generally suffer proportionately in its capacity to love. We find that when the human organism is satisfied in its expectation of love, then it develops as a loving creature with a maximum tolerance for frustration and a minimum need for aggression. Aggression, it turns out, is an acquired, not a *basic*, need. It is a need which is developed in the child that has not had its needs for love adequately satisfied. In such a deprived child, during its critical developmental periods, the need for love may evoke aggressive responses so frequently, that the child may thus be taught aggression instead of the love in which it strives to develop its capacity. Such a child may later, as we know, use aggression whenever it wants anything.

But what is the nature of this behavior customarily called "aggressive"? The usual statement is that it is behavior directed toward the infliction of injury. In this meaning of the term it can safely be said that no human being has ever been born with one iota of aggression in him. In this sense it is doubtful whether any infant under six months of age ever exhibits this kind of hostile aggression. The evidence indicates quite clearly that the destructive element enters, if at all, into the structure of aggression in the later stages of its development. The fact is that Sears and his co-workers [32] found no correlation between early frustration and later preschool aggression in children. They found this not surprising since, by definition, "aggression is taken to be a goal response to instigation to injure" a person, that is, a gratification arising from performing some act causing injury or pain to another. It is absurd to call the taking apart of clocks, the removal of the wings of insects, and the breaking and tearing of objects, in which small children almost invariable indulge, aggressive or destructive behavior. Discovering how things work is an enormously important process in the development of a human being. The best interests of that development are not advanced by treating it as a form of aggression.

The evidence indicates that all personal aggression, whether it be of the early undestructive variety or of the later destructive kind, is almost always the response to love frustrated and the expression of a claim upon others to provide that love. The most extreme forms of destructive aggression, as in murder, are in effect declarations of the position into which the murderer has been forced, causing him to say, "If you will not love me, then I will not love you." Almost always when we witness aggressive behavior, we are observing a demand for love. This is certainly the meaning of the aggressive behavior of those small infants who exhibit it—and it is so at all ages.

Thus understood aggresion is not best met with counteraggresion, but with love—for that is what aggression expresses a need for.[4]

[4] Such aggression is not in itself satisfactory. As Sears and his co-workers conclude in their study of aggression and dependency in young children, "It is clear that the initial stages of the acquisition

It is not human nature but human nurture that
is the cause of human aggression. Human nature is
good, and treated as such leads to goodness. It is for
us to realize, in the light of the accumulated evidence, that being born into the human species means
that the individual so born is capable of becoming
whatever is within the capacity of that individual to
become. The social experience through which the
individual has passed will largely determine whether
he will become a dominantly aggressive or a dominantly loving person or someone betwixt and between. But there can be no doubt that the individual's drives are originally directed toward the
achievement of love, however deformed the process
of achievement may subsequently become. There can
equally be no doubt that the person's drives are
never oriented in a destructive direction, except in
severely disturbed cases, and that such disturbances
are produced principally by cultural factors.

Do let us avoid falling into the error of attributing
to innate nature that which has been produced by
cultural factors. Above all do let us avoid setting up
our prejudices concerning human nature as the in-
eluctable laws of nature. Premature psychosclerosis

of aggression involve no more than the learning of specific adaptive
acts that serve to remove certain kinds of interference. These acts
happen to be destructive or injurious; they may be considered as
instrumental rather than goal response aggression. That is, they
are intended simply to aid in achieving gratification of some other
drive; they are not satisfying in and of themselves. Much of the
interpersonal aggression observed between ages two and four is of
this character, and the true *goal response aggression* becomes no-
ticeable, in many children, only gradually during that period."
R. R. Sears, et al., p. 209, [32].

is to be deplored in the votaries of any discipline in the process of becoming scientific. Reverence for father-figures is important, but so is irreverence. The dignity of an inquirer is not best maintained by adorning himself with a halo of authority from whatever source derived; such dignity Laurence Sterne once defined as a mysterious carriage of the body calculated to conceal the infirmities of the mind. Dignity lies in the maintenance of integrity of mind, in the intellectual honesty which enables one to make the necessary distinctions between hypothesis and fact, rhetoric and argument, prejudice and reason, far-fetched speculations and the laws of nature.

In the words of Robert Browning:

> Truth is within ourselves; it takes no rise
> From outward things, whate'er you may believe:
> There is an inmost centre in us all,
> Where truth abides in fulness; and around,
> Wall within wall, the gross flesh hems it in,
> Perfect and true perception—which is truth;
> A baffling and perverting carnal mesh
> Which binds it, and makes error: and, *"to know"*
> Rather consists in opening out a way
> Whence the imprison'd splendour may dart forth,
> Than in effecting entry for the light
> Supposed to be without.
>
> —"Paracelsus"

It is up to us to recognize, as students of human nature, that we have an important role to fulfill in the re-education of humanity, in releasing that imprisoned splendor which lies within each one of us.

BIBLIOGRAPHY

1. MYRES, J. L., *Political Ideas of the Greeks,* Abingdon Press, New York, 1927, p. 16.

2. RADIN, P., *Primitive Man as a Philosopher,* Appleton, New York, 1927.

3 HONIGMANN, J. J., *Culture and Personality,* Harper, New York, 1954.

4. KLUCKHOHN, C., *The Influence of Psychiatry on Anthropology During the Past One Hundred Years. In One Hundred Years of American Psychiatry,* Columbia University Press, New York, 1944, pp. 589–617; KARDINER, A., and LINTON, R., *The Individual and His Society,* Columbia University Press, New York, 1939; KARDINER, A., LINTON, R., DU BOIS, C., and WEST, J., *The Psychological Frontiers of Society,* Columbia University Press, New York, 1945; KLUCKHOHN C., and LEIGHTON, D., *The Navaho,* Harvard University Press, Cambridge, 1946; LEIGHTON, D., and KLUCKHOHN, C., *Children of the People,* Harvard University Press, Cambridge, 1947; THOMPSON, L., and JOSEPH, A., *The Hopi Way,* University of Chicago Press, Chicago, 1944; KLUCKHOHN, C., MURRAY, H., and SCHNEIDER, D., *Personality: In Nature, Society, and Culture,* Knopf, New York, 1954.

5. SIMMONS, L. W., and WOLFF, H. G., *Social Science in Medicine,* Russell Sage Foundation, New York, 1954; SAUNDERS, L., *Cultural Difference and Medical Care,* Rusell Sage Foundation, New York, 1954; PÉQUIGNOT, H., "Scientific and Social Aspects of Modern Medicine," *Impact,* vol. 5, 1954, pp. 203–259.

6. BREASTED, J. H., *The Dawn of Conscience,* Scribners, New York, 1933; PRITCHARD, J. B., ed., *Ancient Near Eastern Texts,* Princeton University Press, Princeton, N. J., 1950.

7. WINSLOW, O. E., *Jonathan Edwards,* Macmillan, New York, 1940.

8. Quoted from TAYLOR, G. R., *Sex in History,* Vanguard Press, New York, 1954, p. 207.

9. MULLER, H. J., *The Uses of the Past,* Oxford University Press, New York, 1952, p. 160.

10. HOBBES, T., *Leviathan.* Cambridge, 1651.

11. MONTAGU, M. F. ASHLEY, *Darwin, Competition and Cooperation,* Schuman, New York, 1952.

12. HUXLEY, T. H., "The Struggle for Existence: A Programme," *Nineteenth Century,* vol. 23, 1888, pp. 161–180.

13. KEITH, A., *The Place of Prejudice in Civilization,* John Day, New York, 1931.

14. FREUD, S., *Beyond the Pleasure Principle,* Hogarth Press, London, 1922, p. 26.

15. FREUD, S., *An Outline of Psychoanalysis,* Norton, New York, 1949, p. 20.

16. FREUD S., *Beyond the Pleasure Principle,* p. 55.

17. WALLIN, I. E., *Symbionticism and the Origin of Species,* Williams & Wilkins, Baltimore, 1927, p. 58.

18. MONTAGU, M. F. ASHLEY, *The Direction of Human Development,* Harper, New York, 1955.

19. FREUD, S., *Civilization and Its Discontents,* Hogarth Press, London, 1929, p. 86.

20. MENNINGER, K., *Love Against Hate,* Harcourt, Brace, New York, 1942, p. 295.

21. CHILDE, V. G., *What Happened in History,* Mentor Books, New York, 1946, p. 60.

22. SUTTIE, I., *The Origins of Love and Hate,* Julian Press, New York, 1952, p. 31.

23. LOWREY, L. G., "Personality Distortion and Early Institutional Care," *American Journal of Orthopsychiatry,* vol. 10, 1940, pp. 576–585.

24. LEVY, D. M., "Primary Affect Hunger," *American Journal of Psychiatry,* vol 94, 1937, pp. 643–652.

25. GOLDFARB, W., "The Effects of Early Institutional Care on Adolescent Personality," *Journal of Experimental Education,* vol. 12, 1943, pp. 106–129; and many other papers by the same author.

26. BENDER, L., "Genesis of Hostility in Children," *American Journal of Psychiatry,* vol. 105, 1948, pp. 241–245.

27. SPITZ, R., "Hospitalism," *The Psychoanalytic Study of the Child,* vol. 1, 1945, pp. 53–74; and many other papers by the same author.

28. BOWLBY, J., *Maternal Care and Mental Health,* Columbia University Press, New York, 1951.

29. BANHAM, K. M., "The Development of Affectionate Behavior in Infancy," *Journal of Genetic Psychology,* vol. 76, 1950, pp. 283–289.

30. MASLOW, A., *Motivation and Personality,* Harper, New York, 1954.

31. For further references see MONTAGU, M. F. ASHLEY, *The Direction of Human Development,* Harper, New York, 1955.

32. SEARS, R. R., WHITING, J. W. M., NOWLIS, V., and SEARS, P. S., "Some Child-Rearing Antecedents of Aggression and Dependency in Young Children," *Genetic Psychology Monographs,* vol. 47, 1953, pp. 135–234.

10. The Direction of Women's Education

Education is, or should be, a co-operative enterprise, beyond all else an undertaking in the learning of the theory (that is, the science) and the practice (that is, the art) of human life. A most essential part of this process is the art of human relations, and for women it is particularly important, not only that they learn how to relate to men, but also how to persuade men to relate to them. In elementary and high school, girls will have acquired some knowledge of boys—most of it somewhat puzzling—and one would suppose that they would be encouraged to improve upon this knowledge in college. This question may therefore legitimately be posed: Can educational institutions limited to one sex, especially those dedicated to the period when boys are about to turn into men and girls into women, properly perform the functions of education in a realistic manner? A just question, too, is: Is it possible to conceive of genuine education with one half of the human race omitted from the daily experience of it?

Let us not, however, commit the error of assuming that the education of women is best discussed at the college level. It is not, one very cogent reason being that most persons complete their education outside college. There are many other reasons. There are, for example, in our society, different socioeconomic classes. The upper socioeconomic classes (professional people, owners, and managers) produce about 8 per cent of the total number of children in this country, 90 per cent of whom complete high school and go on to college.

The middle classes (minor professional people, small businessmen, clerical and office workers, farmers, foremen, and some skilled workers) produce a little more than 30 per cent of the total number of children, of whom 60 per cent complete high school and 15 per cent go on to college.

The lower classes (skilled, semiskilled, unskilled laborers, and the like) produce about 60 per cent of the children, of whom about 30 per cent go through high school and only 5 per cent enter college.

Clearly, if we are going to speak about the education of our people, the majority are going to be left out if we concentrate our attention on those who are, as the phrase has it, fortunate enough to go to college. Nevertheless, most discussions of this sort focus their attention upon the college student. As a college teacher with a quarter of a century's experience, let me assure you that, so far as genuine education is concerned, by the time the student gets to college it is later than some of us are prepared to think. Not that the college student is a lost soul who is no longer educable, in spite of the opinion of some professors, but the most important part of one's education begins and is completed long before one gets to college. The college years constitute the terminal experience of one's formal education, not its beginning, although for some, indeed, it has proven a beginning—a beginning that was all the more difficult because it came so late.

I want to speak about education for all, for those who will never go to high school or college as well as for those who will do both. And, of course, I want to speak of the role the colleges and the college-educated person can play in the education of humanity. But principally I shall speak here of the direction which I believe the education of women should take. So let us begin by asking a question. It may strike you as a peculiar one—I hope it does.

The question is: Do we, in this country (the same question could be asked in relation to any other country), *educate?* My answer is that we do not. We *instruct.* A very different thing. We instruct and believe that we are educating. This is a confusion which has the most seriously unfortunate consequences; it generally leads to students who exhibit the evidences of inadequate education, in the form of intellectual rickets.

Too often what we tend to regard as progress is, alas, nothing more than the courage of our confusions. The belief in progress, it has been said, is the wine of the present poured out as a libation to the future. Judging the future by the present, which in the past was once the future, it would seem that our domestic educational wines are, perhaps, just a bit too heady and not sufficiently hearty.

The confusion between education and instruction is so serious that it may be predicted that if we go on as we have been doing, in a generation or two there may be no one left who is able to recognize the difference between education and instruction. So before this dire contingency turns into an unhoped-for reality, let us take undisillusioned advantage of the present opportunity to distinguish between the two.

What is instruction? It is the process of conveying information. It is the teaching of the three R's. Is it not substantially true that the larger number of those who pass through our so-called educational institutions emerge equipped with information, which has been pumped into them, but whose richest potentialities have remained uncultivated? It is quite possible to emerge from college a straight-A student and yet be quite uneducated, knowing the price of almost everything and understanding the value of nothing, perfectly equipped with the means to attain a confusion of goals. Let us ask a simple question: Does our contemporary "education" prepare us for living in the contemporary world? I think that the answer is obvious. Apparently not, else this world would not be in the parlous state in which it is at the present moment. Earlier generations were "educated" much as we are being "educated' today, making all allowances for the transference of accumulated methods and some changes in the educational format. Has the world grown any better? In some respects it has, but in many others it has substantially deteriorated. In America, for example, we have the highest murder and crime rates in the world. We have the second highest alcoholic rate, and one of the highest suicide rates. We dropped the atom bomb on two Japanese cities, killing and maiming scores of thousands of human beings. Please remember that I am not drawing up an indictment against any people. I am not blaming anyone. If I were to speak of many other peoples, they, too, would not be found altogether faultless. The inhumanities of the Nazis and the Fascists, whether of Germany, Italy, or the State of Mississippi, are too fresh in the mind for us to forget that some members of the human family are capable of sins against humanity—yes, even in the second half of the twentieth century—which outrank in inhumanity anything that Attila and his Huns ever devised. Our function should be to understand, not to condemn or to condone. To blame is a mark of immaturity, and though it may take a lifetime to learn this, one cannot blame when one understands.

The development of this kind of understanding constitutes an essential part of the educated person's equipment. We have to learn to understand how we got to be the way we are today, and through that understanding, determine how we can improve ourselves and our society nearer to the ideal, the achievable ideal, that we should endeavor, at least, to approximate.

The world of humanity is not in a happy state, and yet we can clearly see, on the distant horizon, the happiness that the greater part of humanity would be able to attain could we but successfully overcome the obstacles which lie in our way.

Let me say at once that I firmly believe that the most important role in overcoming those obstacles will be played by women. In fact, I do not believe that those obstacles can be successfully overcome unless women are prepared to play their necessary role in the remaking of the world of humanity. I believe that the direction of women's education should consist in preparing women to play that role—not one particular class of women, but all women.

This role is a complex one, but it consists in what I regard as its most important phase, in being an educator and active participator in the affairs of humanity. In my understanding of these words, an educator and an active participator in the affairs of humanity mean essentially one and the same thing. Social participation may be regarded as an aspect of the educative process, a continuation of it, in the sense that one not only applies what one has learned in the educative process, but continues to teach others how to enlarge their capacities for participation in the process of making humanity.

What, then, is education? Education is the process of drawing out the potentialities of the individual for being a warm, loving human being who, in the same manner, is then capable of contributing to the creative enlargement of the similar potentialities in others, of contributing to the welfare of others by conferring benefits upon them which enable them not only to live longer but to live more completely. First and foremost, this entails the development of the ability to love, and secondarily, the ability to work. Mental health consists in the ability to love and the ability to work. Insofar as one fails to any extent in the one or the other ability, to that extent is there a failure in one's mental health. Reading, writing, and arithmetic are important, but their importance is secondary compared with the ability to love. The three R's should never be equated in importance with the ability to love, for unless a human being is able to love, no matter how well equipped he may be in the three R's, he is certain to be a tragic failure as a human being. It is not enough to be clever. It is more important to be good. Better still, it is better to be both. Cleverness without goodness has probably been responsible for more damage to the cause of humanity than any other single factor.

There are some charming verses by a distinguished woman, Dame Elizabeth Wordsworth (1840–1932), the first principal of Lady Margaret Hall at Oxford, which make the point:

> If all the good people were clever
> And all clever people were good,
> The world would be nicer than ever
> We thought that it possibly could.
>
> But somehow 'tis seldom or never
> The two hit it off as they should,
> The good are so harsh to the clever,
> The clever so rude to the good!
>
> So friends, let it be our endeavour
> To make each by each understood;
> For few can be good like the clever,
> Or clever, so well as the good.

What we stand so much in need of today is the reconciliation of the good and the clever, the persuasion, moreover, of the good to inquire anew into the foundations of their goodness, and of the clever to be rather more than good, to think more in terms of goodness than in those of cleverness. This is where women can make their major contribution. Women can teach humanity how to be good as well as clever. But before women can do so they have to relearn how to do so. I say "relearn" because all women naturally know, but are more or less caused to forget by the distorted conditioning to which they are exposed in the families into which they are born.

The direction of women's education should be oriented toward the realization that women are the natural teachers of humanity, that women are the mothers of humanity, and that if it is important to be a warm, loving human being, then the best person from whom to learn and develop in one's capacity to love is the mother. The mother stands at the center of humanity since it is she who fundamentally molds the human beings who constitute humanity. The investigations of the behavioral sciences have today given renewed force to the old saying that the hand that rocks the cradle is the hand that rules the world. We need to restore not only the mother to humanity, but also the cradle.

In brief, it has been found that the child is born with certain basic needs which must be adequately satisfied if it is to survive. If it is to develop as a healthy person, the most important of all the needs which must be satisfied is the need to love, which means the need to love others and to develop in one's capacity to love others by being loved. The person naturally endowed to perform this task for the child is the mother. We now have good reason to believe that when the mother adequately performs this task the child grows naturally into health as a seedling grows and blossoms into flower. When the mother inadequately performs this task and, moreover, in the name of "training" more or less systematically visits certain frustrations upon the child, it is likely to suffer considerably from the effects of such inadequate love. The child who has been inadequately loved grows into an inadequately loving person. Such inadequately loving persons make an inadequately loving world. What is wrong with the world today is that it is inadequately loving.

Human beings, especially in the Western world, are confused. They know that something is wrong, and one of their time-honored means of dealing with the situation is to find some adequate scapegoat upon which to expend their hostility: The Russians, the Republicans or the Democrats, or the Communists. Or one resigns oneself to the "fact" that man is by nature simply an ornery, cussed creature and that he will always be getting himself into trouble.

Today there is good scientific evidence indicating that man is not born an ornery, cussed creature—nor, indeed, is he born as some of the textbooks tell us neither good nor evil—and that what he becomes is largely, if not entirely, determined by the experience which he is made to undergo. On the other hand, the evidence indicates that every child is born with a positively organized system of drives which are far from being neutral. These drives are positively organized to function optimally in the realization of the child's potentialities, potentialities to love others and by being loved by them in return, to grow in its capacity for love. Every child wants to live as if to live and love were one. Indeed, every human being is born with all his drives directed toward the realization of his birthright, which is development of his potentialities for being a warm, loving person. As I have already indicated, the mother is both biologically and psychologically best equipped to bring about this development. It is important for all of us to understand this fact and to do everything possible to prepare women in such a manner that they are free and in every way assisted in serving their children, and thus humanity, as they ought.

Now, it might be supposed that at this point I would proceed to recommend that women be educated along those special lines which would bring about this consummation so devoutly to be wished. I shall not quite do that for the simple reason that the education of women, though to some extent it can be separated, is in fact inextricably bound up with the education of men. In the education of men, women will have to be the principal pioneers. The place in which women can begin to do their pioneering is not in the school but in the home, so that by the time the child gets to school, school becomes but a continuation for him of what he has been learning at home—namely, the art of human relations, the art of love.

If women are to be free, men must be freed from the shackles of superstition and custom with which their minds are bound and their ideas relieved of the cobwebs of Time. Men need to learn the facts of life as well as women—only more so. Men need to learn what the meaning of love is, they need to learn how to love, and they need to learn the facts concerning the nature of women and the nature of men. It has been said that women are so different from men that about the only thing they have in common is the species. This may or may not be an exaggeration, but everyone agrees that women are to some extent different from men, and there are some who read the evidence as showing that the natural differences are almost entirely in favor of the female.[1] Men need to learn the simple truth that women are biologically superior to men because women are the biologically more valuable part of the species capital. It is as simple as that, and this law holds true for virtually the whole of animated nature.

It is perhaps an illuminating commentary upon the age in which we live that it is necessary for me to pause in order to explain the statement that women are biologically the more valuable part of the species capital. I mean by this statement that in virtue of the biological necessity that women have to gestate children 266½ days on the average, during this period females are the most valuable part of the species, for unless they survive and bring their pregnancy to a successful conclusion, the species will not be continued. In addition, when a child is born, and for several years thereafter, it is the mother who will nurture it and attend to its needs until it can shift for itself. During the period of gestation the mother must be able to resist all the assaults and insults of the environment; she must, in short be constitutionally stronger than the male—and that she is. A woman normally gives birth to but a single child after a gestation period of almost ten lunar months, where-

[1] M. F. Ashley Montagu, *The Natural Superiority of Women,* Macmillan, New York, 1953.

as during this period a single male can be the father of many children, only one male being necessary for such multiple paternity. Thus, for every female, literally hundreds of males could be dispensed with and the population still maintained in biologic equilibrium. On the other hand, many women of childbearing capacity are necessary if the population is to be maintained and continued.

It is principally for the reason that the female is the biological conserver of the race of humanity that she has been endowed with greater constitutional strength than the male.

If we are to rely upon the psychological tests and upon the tests of experience, it can no longer be seriously doubted that women are at least as intelligent as men and that in virtually all areas of human endeavor, what men can do, women can also do.

Upon such grounds, and upon all others that have been adequately studied, the myths concerning women need to be dispelled. Women as well as men need to learn the truth about these myths. Our aim should not be to establish the supremacy of one sex over another, but rather, by enabling both sexes to learn the facts about themselves in relation to each other, to enable them to realize their potentialities and responsibilities in behalf of humanity as its teachers. For it is principally the quality of the mother's relation to the child that determines the kind of humanity of which the child will later be capable. I would suggest that the principal task of our educational institutions in educating is to prepare them in the theory and practice of being mothers. At least until all parents know how to make loving human beings

out of their children, such teaching should be assumed by the schools. And I would commence not
at the elementary school level but at the nursery
school level. Toward this end, among others, I would
make the nursery school part of the educational
system of the land. By this means the home and
school would be brought together in the complementary task of educating the child, and not least
important, the further education of the mother and
to some extent the father. From the very first, the
emphasis should be on the art of human relations,
which is nothing more than the art of loving. Thus,
teachers should be specially chosen for their ability
to love, this being the primary requirement in the
equipment of the teacher. Where anything that is
taught has any relation to human life, then it should
be taught within the matrix of love. The referent in
the education of the child should always be how
what is being taught contributes toward the development of the child as a healthy human being—to
repeat, health consists in the ability to love and the
ability to work.

What I am suggesting, in fact, is nothing less than
a revolution in our attitudes toward education; I am
suggesting that we regard education as the drawing
out, nourishment, and development of the potentialities of every individual for being a loving human
being who co-operatively realizes himself in relation
to the welfare of his fellows and thus of his own
best self. According to this view, the principal purpose of our schools should be education in human
relations by drawing out and nourishing the innate
capacities of every human being for relatedness. The

teaching of the three R's should constitute a second-ary but complementary process in the interest of rendering more efficient the functioning of such relatedness.

It seems to me that it will be women predominantly who will be the pioneers in achieving this change in the educational process, and it therefore behooves our high school and college educators to prepare women for the task of bringing this change about, by making all the relevant evidence, materials, and techniques for participation available to them. Insofar as formal education is concerned, I would institute courses at the outset of high school, to be continued throughout college, on the social biology of the sexes. Such courses would cover the biological, psychological, and social differences which exist between the sexes, with a view to making each individual aware of his particular nature as well as that of members of the opposite sex, and aware of the roles which each will be required to play in life. It is especially important to teach the male to understand, rather more soundly than he has in the past, what to him has been the mystery of all mysteries, namely, the female. The mystery of the female is merely an evidence of the transparency of the male. All the more reason, therefore, for understanding that part of the education of the female must be her preparation for the education of the male in the art of being human—otherwise however we educate females, their education will remain imperfect and be marred by the fact that they exhibit the traits of a group in reaction to a dominant group, the males. In other words, a large part of the psychology of women, and particularly that part of it for which they have been

particularly condemned and derided by men, represents the reaction of women to both the devices and
the requirements of men. It is for this reason that
an important part of the education of women must
be devoted to the education of men; until men are
free of the myths that bind them, women will not
be free to be themselves. It is in coeducational institutions that such education is best achieved.

I would make education for motherhood an indispensable part of the development of all females,
whether they are eventually going to raise a family
or not. It is good, and it should be necessary, for all
women to understand what being a mother means.
Whether a woman becomes a biological mother or
not, the really important thing is for all women to
develop their maternal, their naturally protecting
and conserving, attitudes of mind. Of these the world
will always stand much in need. The natural con-
servers of humanity are the women of the world,
and this they will always be. A society which insuffi-
ciently recognizes this truth seriously endangers the
possibilities of its own perpetuation. How many of
our educational institutions ever give their students
a course in the meaning of motherhood? I mean not
only the women, but the men? The men, perhaps,
stand more in need of learning the true meaning of
motherhood, of what is means to be a woman, than
the women do; for the latter almost always retain
something of this understanding in spite of the worst
efforts of our technological culture to mechanize even
the process of maternity.

To what extent can one legitimately think of the
education of women as something apart from the

education of men, that there is one kind of education for women and another kind for men? Of course women should not be educated as if they were going to be men. They should be educated as persons who happen to be women, and who, as such, are going to play the most important of all roles in society, that of mothers. The status of motherhood must be raised so that it is esteemed for what it is, the most important of all professions, and our educational institutions should provide all women with the special opportunities which would enable them to learn to conduct themselves as well as possible in this, the most underprivileged of professions. The women who did not marry and had no children would not be spending their time needlessly in acquiring such competence, for they would be able to utilize it in extending the attitudes of the loving mother to all with whom they came into association.

I see this as the most significant of all the directions in which women's education of the immediate future should proceed. When women are educated to be, among other things, good mothers, we may look forward to a general improvement in the lot of humanity. Not that by this means humanity will all at once attain perfection, but certainly by this means we shall stand a much better chance of approximating it than we do at present.[2]

This I regard as the primary and fundamental basis of women's education. The second direction in which women's education should be oriented is in the sphere of social participation. Women must be

[2] See M. F. Ashley Montagu, *The Direction of Human Development*, Harper, New York, 1955.

convinced that they are really significant human beings in their own right, that they are not merely
second-class or third-rate men, that they are not
members of a minority or inferior group, that they
have rights, privileges, and obligations, and that they
should enjoy the exercise of them as responsible
members of the community. Women have already
abundantly shown how ably they can function in
virtually every sphere which was formerly regarded
as sacrosanct to the male. Through such organiza-
tions as the League of Women Voters, the Parent-
Teachers Association, and numerous similar bodies,
they have shown themselves a strong power for good
that gives great promise for the future. Should anyone whisper sotto voce, "Yes, but what about the
Daughters of the American Revolution?" we can only
say in defense that after all it was that poor demented
soul George III who was responsible for them by
exhibiting all the masculine vices in their extremest
forms. Of course our interest should be not in the
daughters so much as in the mothers of the American
revolution—the revolution that should occur in each
generation in the minds of our citizens, the revolution of progress toward the attainment of humanity.
As Nathaniel Hawthorne put it, "Human nature will
not flourish, any more than a potato, if it be planted
and replanted, for too long a series of generations,
in the same worn-out soil."

Women must be educated for greater participation
in the government of their societies. By "societies"
I mean the local community, the state, the nation,
and the community of nations. In all of these relations women have already shown their mettle, and

there can be not the least doubt that increasing numbers of women will participate in government at all these levels as time goes on. Our problem as educators is how we are going to help women to do so in increasing numbers and with all the neccessary efficiency? How are we going to deal with the fact that for many mothers the obligations of family life render it extremely difficult for them to participate in anything other than the affairs of the immediate family?

Let us attempt an answer to the second question first. In a land in which most mothers are likely to be deprived of the advantages of domestic help, the bringing up of children is going to be a full-time job. Most young mothers with several small children to care for, work an average of sixteen hours a day, seven days a week. All that most of them will have time for during these years will be recovery from the accumulated exhaustion of looking after a family— that is, if we continue with the kind of attitudes toward human beings that we at present exhibit. If, on the other hand, we believe that it is to the advantage of everyone concerned for young parents to enjoy their families in a relaxed manner, enabling each parent to participate more actively in the affairs of their society than is at the present time possible for them, then we must devise some means for making this a possibility.

It has been suggested that a four-hour working day, on a voluntary basis, be made available to all men who have become fathers, and for all women who are mothers. The mother, of course, usually stays with her children for the first few years, but her task would be greatly lightened by having the father who works four hours a day home with her for the greater part of her day to share with her in the privileges and obligations of parenthood. Not only would there be no decrease in the father's salary upon this arrangement, but by a system of family allowances, administered by the state, the income of the family would actually be increased. By means of this proposed arrangement, each of the parents could be at home together with their children for a good part of the day, or one parent could be away for a part of the day while the other was at home with the children. All sorts of variations could, of course, be played upon this domestic theme.

Is such a scheme feasible in our society, it will be asked? I believe it is, and I also believe that it would greatly enrich our society in humanity as well as in material wealth. But the only way to find out is to try it. With the co-operation of employers it would not be in the least difficult to put such a plan to the test of practical living. Certainly, the father needs to participate more than he does at the present time in the experience of bringing up his children, while his wife needs a little more freedom than she at present enjoys from that experience, so that she may be all the more efficient in dealing with it. Until we have developed some such arrangement as I have suggested, I do not think that we shall fully master this problem. But until that time, while working to bring such a condition about, it is indispensably necessary so to educate women that they are able to deal with their domestic problems in as efficient a manner as posible, so that the needs of the family are satisfied and the needs of the wife and mother, as a person and a citizen, are also satisfied.

Courses toward this end could be successfully instituted at the high school and college levels. The dilemma of being caught between family and a career can, in most cases, be happily resolved. This is the dilemma in which thousands of women find themselves hopelessly involved, yet we do little through our educational facilities to resolve it. Are the blind leading the blind? Is it possible that our educators need to be educated in the relevant facts concerning the nature of human nature as it differentially expresses itself in the sexes?

Let us return to the matter of the education of women for greater participation in government and the professions, as well as in the world in general. In spite of the fact that there are nearly two million more women in this country than there are men, there are only 16 women in Congress—1 in the Senate and 15 in the House—as compared with 515 men. Is not this a striking example of disproportionate representation? Women surely have at least as valuable qualities to contribute to government as men. As a scientific observer of the human scene, I believe that women have far more valuable qualities to bring to government than men, among these being the qualities of love, sympathy, compassion, and the desire to conserve. These are qualities of which the world will always stand much in need—and never, perhaps, more than at the present time. Our educators of women should recognize this fact and orient the education of women in such a manner as to encourage them, by providing them with the knowledge and the confidence, which will eventually lead more and more women into public life.

The midwives of the future are going to be women working together with men—men alone will never solve the human problem any more satisfactorily than they have up to the present time. The culturally induced masculine qualities of self-assertiveness, aggressiveness, and bluntness are not the qualities the world stands most in need of. I submit that the qualities which humanity will always find adaptively the most valuable are love, sympathy, compassion, and the desire to conserve—and these are predominantly the feminine qualities. I am convinced that insofar as humanity has failed to achieve a happier state on earth, it is in large part due to the fact that women have not been afforded the opportunity for active participation in the government of human affairs.

Profesor Kate Hevner Mueller has recently written, "Woman, even more than man, must express herself creatively in some service to society, and must have approbation and recognition *from other individuals* for this contribution."[3]

Being a good mother is the greatest service a woman can perform to her society, and this also includes being a good wife to her husband, which as every woman—I mean every married woman—knows, often largely consists in being a good mother to him. The ·making of good citizens is largely dependent upon the manner in which the mother makes good human beings of her children. When that, the most impor-

[3] Kate Hevner Mueller, *Educating Women for a Changing World*, University of Minnesota Press, Minneapolis, 1955, p. 61.

tant of all tasks, has been satisfactorily completed, she still has many years of useful life to contribute creatively to her society—and every society should afford her ample opportunities for doing so. That, also, is an understanding in which our society needs to be educated. Not only women, but men especially, need to be educated to understand this, that in the home, in government, in the professions, and in the world in general, women have a valuable and important role to play. Man-made, and also some women-made, traditional prejudices need to undergo re-examination and dissolution. In this task our colleges have a leading role to play.

In a democratic society in which the ideas of the worth of the individual and the contribution he has to make on the whole are so often reiterated, it should be recognized that women have equal rights with men; not the least important part of a liberal education should consist in the preparation of both sexes in the manner in which those rights can best be realized.

When each sex is clearly acquainted with the role that it is destined to play in life, together they will bring into being those conditions which will activate their complementary abilities in the reciprocal contribution to each other's development of their children. They will adjust to each other more easily and to the conditions of life to which adjustment must also be made. The problem, of course, is to adjust the conditions of life to one's own needs as closely as is compatible with the welfare of the group as a whole. It is such problems as these that our colleges should be working on and our educators thinking about. It seems to me that we touch here upon the very essence of the problem of education, the human problem, the problem of adjusting the sexes to each other so that each may fulfill itself with the help of the other, and the problem of adjusting our social arrangements to the needs of warm, loving human beings. It is not human beings who require to be adjusted to society, but rather society which requires to be adjusted to human beings, for society is essentially man's means of meeting his needs. In order that those needs shall be properly satisfied it is necessary to understand those needs. Have we understood them? I think not.[4] Yet the knowledge is available. It has, however, become so recently available that there has been little time either for its diffusion or assimilation.

The faculties of our colleges can spend their time no more profitably than by acquainting themselves with what science has revealed during the last fifty years concerning the nature of human nature, and by helping their students to make this knowledge part of themselves so that they can apply it with the wisdom that will come of its application.

As a final word, I should like to say, in the modern version of an apothegm of Oliver Wendell Holmes, that I have never yet seen a man, distinguishable from a gorilla, that some good woman could not shape a human being out of.

[4] See Erich Fromm, *The Sane Society*, Rinehart, New York, 1955.

11. Anthropology and World History

History is made by man, and anthropology is the study of man's own history from his earliest origins to the present day. For the teacher of world history, anthropology should be an indispensable study, which will add depth and greater objectivity to his understanding of world history, and will arm him with facts and viewpoints which should assist him greatly in the teaching of his subject.

The anthropologist studies the history of each people as a self-consistent whole. One of the principal lessons learned by students of anthropology is that of cultural relativity or the ability to evaluate the behavior and institutions of another people in terms of its own social organization without introducing the distortion of one's own biases as a member of a different culture. Each people must be understood in terms of its own history of experiences and not that of the external observer. Anthropology shows why it is unsound to compare different peoples and their way of life, their cultures, without first clearly comprehending the differences in the history of their experience. These are most valuable lessons for the teacher of world history. His ability to convey such lessons to his pupils may well play a substantial part in determining the future course of world events.

As a distinguished anthropologist, Clyde Kluckhohn, recently remarked, "Anthropology holds up a great mirror to man and lets him look at himself in his infinite variety." It is an understanding of that infinite variety which, more than anything else, the world stands in need of today. In order to understand the nature of that variety, it is necessary to understand the nature of man.

What Is the Nature of Human Nature?

Why Study the Nature of Human Nature? For a variety of reasons. Because (1), when we understand the nature of man it becomes possible to distinguish those of his functions which are inborn from those which are acquired. It then becomes possible to answer such questions as: Are the achievements of different peoples due to innate differences, or to differences in history of experience to which they have been exposed? What makes one people aggressive and another submissive? Are social differences within the same people based on natural or acquired conditions? Is war inevitable because war is an instinctive urge of man? Because (2), in the light of such understanding it becomes possible to destroy misconceptions relating to the nature of human nature which give rise to false ideologies, international rivalries and conflicts, and political and social policies which are unsound, socially harmful, and personally disintegrating. Because (3), a correct view of human nature enables us to view the history of man in all his complex variety in deeper perspective, or dimensionally. At the present day the false views of human nature which are pretty universally held cause us to evaluate historical as well as contemporary developments in terms of our own narrow culture bias, rather than in the light of the dimensions of human nature. These dimensions are man's organic nature, the socialization provided by his human cultivators, and the history of experience undergone by his cultural group.

Up to the very recent present and the advent of modern anthropology, the belief had grown that human nature differs racially, ethnically, nationally, and even among social classes of the same people. Hence, it became a simple matter to account for the differences in human nature. Since, as everyone still seems to know, "you can't change human nature," it became quite obvious that the peoples who had conquered others during the history of the world were "superior" to those whom they had defeated, and world history could be regarded as a continuation of natural history. This conception of human nature gained ascendancy in the nineteenth century with the rise (in the midst of the industrial revolution and a rampant imperialism) of the Darwinian theory of evolution and its doctrines of natural selection, "the struggle for existence," and "the survival of the fittest." Intellectually honest men and distinguished scientists could persuade themselves and others that the virtual enslavement of "the lower classes," the exploitation of the lands of "inferior peoples" and their eventual supplantation by the "white race," were not only biologically justifiable but the clear judgment of Nature (with a capital N). In recent years we have witnessed the culmination of this belief in the tragic events which followed the rise of Hitler.

It is seen, then, that ideas concerning the nature of human nature are not of purely theoretical interest, but that they have the most important bearing upon the actual lives and welfare of human beings—everywhere. They determine public and national policies and the fate of millions of human beings.

Hence, Let Us Consider Briefly What the Anthropologist Has to Say About Human Nature. Man is born with certain basic needs or physiological urges which must be satisfied if the organism is to survive. These needs are: oxygen, food, liquids, sleep, bowel and bladder emptying, rest, activity, and avoidance of pain and danger. The ways in which these needs are satisfied differ substantially in different cultures. In socializing the child each culture serves to organize the child's needs in such a manner as to cause it to expect its satisfactions in a particular style and to fulfill its duties to others in the manner expected of it.

In the past the approach to the problem of the nature of man has been unsound. The question asked usually took the simple form: What is the nature of man? Instead, the correct phrasing of the question should be: What is it that has been organized or built into man? Man is the animal beyond all others that has been freed from biologically predetermined responses and therefore must learn those responses which have so often been miscalled "human nature." Human nature is the pattern of responses which is inculcated into the organism by the tradition of the group through the agency of its parents and teachers. Allowing for the fact that organically the potentialities of no two individuals are ever quite the same, the basic pattern of responses which all individuals learn within any culture are recognizably similar, and different from that which exists in all other cultural groups.

It is this variety in cultural conditioning which accounts for the different forms which human nature assumes in different cultures. Basically there are no significant differences in the organic potentialities of different groups of mankind. We must therefore conclude that so-called differences in human nature are in fact differences in second nature, the nature which is artificially developed in response to the stimulation of a particular kind of cultural experience. It will depend entirely upon the kind of socialization the child has undergone whether his human nature will be that of a Congo pygmy or that of a Norwegian fisherman. Children of one ethnic group who are socialized in the milieu of another develop the nature peculiar to the group in which they have been socialized. There are many records of white children who were captured by American Indians and raised as Indians, who became so completely Indianized that it was only by being informed of their origin that others became aware of their real extraction. In the United States we observe Japanese-Americans becoming completely Americanized within a few generations, while Negroes have lost every bit of their African cultural heritage.

It should always be remembered that so far as human behavior is concerned the one thing natural to man is to be artificial—artificial in the sense that man's behavior is made up of learned, acquired abstractions and motor activities calculated to make him comfortable in the world in which he finds himself. Human nature, in short, is what man makes of man or, perhaps more accurately, what he makes of the children.

What Should Be Put into Our World History Courses to Clear Up the Prevailing Misconceptions Concerning the Nature of Man? Many anthropological studies of nonliterate peoples[1] are now available which are calculated to show how great differences in so-called human nature are produced in adjacent cultures. There are two fundamental source books on this phase of the subject: Ruth Benedict's *Patterns of Culture,* and Margaret Mead's *From the South Seas.* Material from these two books could, perhaps, be incorporated early in the course in the unit on prehistoric and nonliterate peoples.

A second phase of the subject, which might be placed in the same unit, should deal with the fact that certain basic institutions are found among all human groups. Here four books are indispensable, namely, Bronislaw Malinowski's *A Scientific Theory of Culture,* George Murdock's *Social Structure,* La Barre's *The Human Animal,* and Ashley Montagu's

[1] The phrase "primitive peoples" should be avoided.

The Direction of Human Development. These works answer the questions: (1) What are basic needs of man, and how does culture arise out of their satisfactions, and (2) What determines the nature of certain basic human institutions, and what institutions are most often found in clusters and why?

The following references will be of value for those who wish to read further on the nature of man:

BENEDICT, RUTH, *Patterns of Culture,* Mentor Books, New York, 1946.

CHILDE, V. GORDON, *Man Makes Himself,* Oxford University Press, New York, 1936.

CHILDE, V. GORDON, *What Happened in History,* Penguin Books, Baltimore, 1946.

GILLIN, JOHN, *The Ways of Men,* Appleton-Century, New York, 1948.

HONIGMANN, JOHN, *Culture and Personality,* Harper, New York, 1954.

KARDINER, ABRAM, *The Individual and His Society,* Columbia University Press, New York, 1939.

KLUCKHOHN, CLYDE, *Mirror for Man,* Whittlesey House, New York, 1949.

KLUCKHOHN, CLYDE, MURRAY, HENRY A., and SCHNEIDER, DAVID, eds., *Personality in Nature, Society, and Culture,* Knopf, New York, 1954.

LA BARRE, WESTON, *The Human Animal,* University of Chicago Press, Chicago, 1954.

LINTON, RALPH, *The Cultural Background of Personality,* Appleton-Century, New York, 1945.

LINTON, RALPH, ed., *The Science of Man in the World Crisis,* Columbia University Press, New York, 1944.

MALINOWSKI, BRONISLAW, *A Scientific Theory of Culture,* University of North Carolina Press, Chapel Hill, 1944.

MEAD, MARGARET, *From the South Seas,* Morrow, New York, 1939.

MONTAGU, M. F. ASHLEY, *The Biosocial Nature of Man,* Grove Press, New York, 1956.

MONTAGU, M. F. ASHLEY, *The Direction of Human Development,* Harper, New York, 1955.

MURDOCK, GEORGE P., *Social Structure,* Macmillan, New York, 1949.

WHAT DO WE KNOW ABOUT RACES

Why Study the Subject of Race? Largely to clear up the misconceptions which have mushroomed up about the most dangerous myth of the twentieth century. Something called "race" is generally conceived to be the prime determiner of all the important traits of body and mind, of character and personality of human beings and nations. This something called "race" is further believed to be a fixed and unchangeable part of the germ plasm which, transmitted from generation to generation, unfolds in each people as a typical expression of personality and culture. Since the creators of this view of "race" belonged to the white division of mankind, they claimed that the white race was superior to all others. Lately, in pre-Hitlerite and in Hitler's Germany, it was claimed that the German people belonged to an exceptionally pure branch of the white race which had been largely responsible for most of the achievements of Western civilization. All of these claims are utterly false.

What Should Be Put into Our World History Courses to Clear Up These Misconceptions? Three phases of this subject should be considered as follows:

1. All mankind is derived from a common ancestry, and all belong to the same single species *Homo sapiens*. There are four major groups of mankind: the Negroid, the Mongoloid, the Archaic Caucasoid, and the Caucasoid. These major groups number a large variety of different physical types which are best called "ethnic groups," rather than "races." The differentiation of these ethnic groups has been brought about by such factors as isolation, mutation of genes, random fixation of genes or genetic drift (i.e. the Sewall Wright effect), natural selection, hybridization, and possibly sexual selection.

Every ethnic group is much mixed. There never were and there are not any "pure races." The history of man has, from the earliest times, been one of migration and intermingling. If we would understand what has happened in the ethnic history of mankind in the past, all we have to do is to look about us in the present. Every nation of the modern world is made up of a large number of intermingled ethnic elements. The most recent and possibly outstanding example of such a nation is the United States, wherein, with few exceptions, every ethnic group in the world is represented. Hawaii is another contemporary example. Ancient Greece, Britain, France, Germany, Italy,[2] and the countries of Latin America are well-documented examples of extensive ethnic intermingling. (Reference should be made to the works of Adams, Coon, Day, Diller, Shapiro, and Ashley Montagu for studies on "race mixture" both

[2] The students might well study the effects of Hannibal's stay in Italy on population mixture.

in the past and at the present day.) From the stand-point of the biologist and the student of civilization, "race mixture" has had nothing but good effects upon man as an organism and as a civilized being. (See the writings of Castle and Angel.)

2. The differences between the varieties of man-kind are minor, the likenesses major. The differences for the most part, if not entirely, represent adaptive changes which have been favored by natural selec-tion. The likenesses are due to common ancestry. The evidence, as set out by Dobzhansky and Ashley Montagu, indicates that the one factor which has had the highest survival value in the evolution of man has been the general trait of plasticity or the ability to make more or less rapid adjustment to changing conditions, i.e., to profit from experience and education. The effect of natural selection in man has probably been to render genotypic differ-ences in personality traits in different ethnic groups relatively unimportant compared to their phenotypic (expressed or visible) plasticity.

In spite of innumerable investigations calculated to discover whether there exist any innate mental differences between the ethnic groups of man, all the evidence indicates that there are no such significant differences. Such differences as are found can usually be explained by differences in such conditions as culture, socioeconomic environment, and the kind of schooling experience. For example, American Ne-groes living in the North generally rate significantly higher on intelligence tests than do Negroes living in the South. Army intelligence tests of World War I show that the Negroes from certain Northern States did better on intelligence tests than the whites from many Southern States.

3. All ethnic groups have made contributions, of which many people could be justly proud, to the great common stock of human knowledge. Each ethnic group has made social discoveries and invented devices which through diffusion have spread to many other peoples and thus benefited them. Civilization is the product of innumerable different peoples. Not one has a monopoly on any of those contributions, for though a contribution may be originally their own invention or discovery, when it is adopted by other peoples it is usually improved and modified by the adopters. Important works giving much data on the origin and diffusion of inventions and discoveries by nonliterate and other peoples are those of Herskovits, Linton, and Lips.

Those who wish to read further about race will find the following books and articles most instructive:

ADAMS, ROMANZO C., *Interracial Marriage in Hawaii*, Macmillan, New York, 1937.

ANGEL, JOHN L., "Social Biology of Greek Culture Growth," *American Anthropologist*, vol. 48, 1946, pp. 493–533.

CASTLE, WILLIAM E., "Biological and Social Consequences of Race Crossing," *American Journal of Physical Anthropology*, vol. 9, 1926, pp. 145–146.

CASTLE, WILLIAM E., "Race Mixture and Physical Disharmonics," *Science*, vol. 71, 1930, pp. 603–606.

COON, CARLETON S., *The Races of Europe*, Macmillan, New York, 1939.

COON, CARLETON S., GARN, STANLEY M., and BIRDSELL, JOSEPH B., *Races*, C. C. Thomas, Springfield, Ill., 1950.

DAY, CAROLINE B., *A Study of Some Negro-White Families in the United States*, Peabody Museum, Harvard University, Cambridge, 1932.

DILLER, AUBREY, *Race Mixture Among the Greeks Before Alexander*, Illinois Studies in Language and Literature, vol. xx, University of Illinois, Urbana, 1937.

DOBZHANSKY, THEODOSIUS, and MONTAGU, M. F. ASHLEY, "Natural Selection and the Mental Capacities of Mankind," *Science*, vol. 105, 1947, pp. 587–590.

HERSKOVITS, MELVILLE J., *Man and His Works*, Knopf, New York, 1948.

LINTON, RALPH, *The Study of Man*, Appleton-Century, New York, 1936.

LIPS, JULIUS, *The Origin of Things*, A. A. Wyn, New York, 1947.

MONTAGU, M. F. ASHLEY, "The Intelligence of Northern Negroes and Southern Whites in the First World War," *American Journal of Psychology*, vol. 68, 1945, pp. 161–188.

MONTAGU, M. F. ASHLEY, *An Introduction to Physical Anthropology*, 2nd ed., C. C. Thomas, Springfield, Ill., 1951.

MONTAGU, M. F. ASHLEY, *Man's Most Dangerous Myth: The Fallacy of Race*, 3rd ed., Harper, New York, 1952.

MONTAGU, M. F. ASHLEY, *Statement on Race*, 2nd ed., Abelard-Schuman, New York, 1952.

SHAPIRO, HARRY L., *Descendants of the Mutineers of Bounty*, Memoirs of the Bernice P. Bishop Museum, vol. ix, Honolulu, 1929.

What Have Been the Really Great Cultural Mutations in History?

Why Study Cultural Mutations? Largely in order to clear up the misconception that modern man has made the great discoveries of history, and that only modern man (and particularly modern man from Western civilization) has been bright enough to make such discoveries or inventions.

What Should Be Put into World History Courses to Prevent the Development of or to Eliminate This Misconception? Emphasis should be placed on prehistoric times and on the two great cultural revolutions of those times: (1) the discovery of agriculture and the domestication of animals, and (2) the urban revolution.

The planting, cultivation, and improvement by selection of edible grasses, roots, and trees, and the domestication of animals constituted the first great change in man's way of life since the beginning of his history. These discoveries made possible the increase of population which is still continuing today. It is obvious that food-producing economy could support a much larger population than a food-gathering and hunting economy such as existed throughout the vast eras of the ice ages. The food-gatherer and hunter was a nomad. Food production and domestication of animals necessitated permanent settlement and thus the growth of villages. Greater leisure and new needs produced craftsmen who could make new and better tools, such as the hoe, the plow, the loom, the spinning wheel, the wheeled cart, the sailing boat, and finally copper and bronze tools. "In no period in history," remarks Childe, "till the days of Galileo was progress in knowledge so rapid or far-reaching discoveries so frequent."

The second revolution in man's way of life followed naturally upon the development of the food-producing economy—namely, urbanization. Urbanization first developed in Egypt and Mesopotamia where the rainfall is low and the necessity for water therefore high. It was discovered that the flood waters of the Nile and of the Tigris and Euphrates rivers could be controlled and put to work. Irrigation canals and ditches could be dug and dikes and reservoirs built. Such projects required the co-operative labor of many people working together. Greater organization was soon required for control over the use of water. Population increased, and the city developed to accommodate the needs of an increasing population. Craftsmen and artisans were encouraged to specialize. Administrators, technicians, judges, priests, and many new roles were created in order to take care of the increased complexity of living in this new kind of world. Geometry, arithmetic, writing, astronomy, and the calendar gradually developed to meet the demands of the new economy. In brief, the fundamental discoveries and inventions upon which modern civilization is based were made by the peoples of the Near East before the dawn of the Christian era.

Invention and discovery depend upon the demands of an economy which is developing, and which therefore requires new ideas and new instruments with which to deal with new problems. Where there is no need, inventions and discoveries will either not be made, or if they are, they will not be used. Ancient Greece is a good example. The Greeks were superlatively good at almost everything but mechanical devices. Their lack of interest in machines was due to the fact that the Greek economy was based on slavery, the slaves supplying all the necessary energy for the requirements of that economy. Hence, while some ingenious machines were invented, they were treated rather as curiosities or playthings than as economically important contributions.

For those who are interested in reading further on the great cultural mutations of history, the following books will be of use:

BRAIDWOOD, ROBERT J., *Prehistoric Men,* Chicago Natural History Museum, Popular Series, Anthropology Number 37, Chicago, 1948.

CHILDE, V. GORDON, *The Dawn of European Civilization,* Knopf, New York, 1948.

CHILDE, V. GORDON, *Man Makes Himself,* Oxford University Press, New York, 1936.

CHILDE, V. GORDON, *What Happened in History,* Penguin Books, Baltimore, 1946.

COON, CARLETON S., *The Story of Man,* Knopf, New York, 1954.

HOWELLS, W. W., *Back of History,* Doubleday, New York, 1954.

LINTON, RALPH, *The Tree of Culture,* Knopf, New York, 1955.

TURNER, RALPH, *The Great Cultural Traditions,* 2 vols, McGraw-Hill, New York, 1941.

WHAT ARE SOME OF THE MAJOR BARRIERS TO OUR UNDERSTANDING OF OTHER CIVILIZATIONS?

Why Study the Nature of These Barriers? Because of the need to evaluate our own ideas in an objective manner in order to secure greater progress in satisfying the needs of mankind. Our minds are not open and we are unable to understand the viewpoints of other peoples. As a result, we are unable to work out sound relations with them.

Mankind can be rescued from the effects of closed-mindedness by training in open-mindedness. The criteria of the open mind are alertness, interest in the ways in which people make up their minds, skill in analyzing the influence of one's personal interests, prejudices, and allegiances, and skill in the processes of critical thinking. The world history teacher is in a strategic position to teach the methods and the advantages of open-mindedness by exemplification through his teaching.

One of the greatest barriers to our understanding of other peoples and civilizations is our own cultural bias or ethnocentrism. This is a fault which we share with every other people, and probably with every people that has ever existed. Every human group tends to regard itself, at least in some way, as superior to all others. This is not a natural or inborn trait but the result of group conditioning. The function of a truly civilized community should be to de-condition its people of such tendencies, and condition them to be interested in other peoples, and to understand their values.

What Should Be Put into Our World History

Courses to Help Students See Cultural Bias? Emphasis should be placed upon the history of our own values, their sources and their development. The evidence should be given for the fact that our own system of values is based upon, and largely derived from, Assyrian, Hebraic, and Graeco-Roman moral and secular codes, plus the modifications introduced by our own way of life. The interaction of these ways of life to form our own could be traced through ethical codes, legal systems, religions, and principles of government. The discovery, settlement, and conquest of America may serve as an excellent illustration of the way in which values become modified and substantially changed by the necessities involved in the pioneering of a new country and the development of a "frontier spirit," in this case, "rugged American individualism." The emphasis upon success in our culture may be traced as an outgrowth of the immigrant-pioneering spirit, which causes parents to socialize their children "to do better" than their parents. Equality of opportunity for oneself becomes a dominant, overt value, though covertly we believe in the inequality of opportunity and of men. The historical sources of these and other of our values should be fully explored.

Values are attitudes of mind. Values represent judgments as to the manner in which the best adjustment may be made to certain conditions. All peoples obviously must have values. It should be made clear that since the conditions of life, the history, of each people have differed, the value system of each people therefore differs accordingly. Once this concept of historical or cultural relativity is grasped, it becomes possible to understand *why* the values of other peoples differ from our own. This can best be demonstrated by showing how some other peoples got their values. Ruth Benedict's *Patterns of Culture* is invaluable here. Study of the great cultures outside Western civilization, those of China and India in particular, could most efficiently serve to develop a more balanced view of the quality and value of value systems other than our own.

All through the course, the world history teacher should emphasize the historically relativistic viewpoint, the viewpoint which causes one to look at things from other viewpoints, and to examine them in the light of what we know about man's needs and the adaptations which under different conditions he makes to them.

The teacher can include some of the practical applications of anthropology during the last war as an example of ways in which cultural relativity can be of value in promoting understanding between peoples. Immediately prior to and during World War II the United States government called into its service many anthropologists to advise on our relations with other peoples. By placing written analyses of the value systems and the basic patterns of culture and personality of all the peoples with whom we were likely to have any relations in the hands of the army and the government, anthropologists greatly facilitated the handling of situations which would otherwise have been difficult. Anthropologists enabled our government officials, our intelligence service, and our armed men to understand and get along with people upon whom they had never previously set eyes and of